Grimoire Dehara

Kaimana

Grimoire Dehara

Kaimana

Storm Constantine

Megalithica Books
Stafford England

Grimoire Dehara: Kaimana
By Storm Constantine © 2005
2nd edition 2011

Story quotes in this book are works of fiction. All the characters
and events portrayed in these extracts are fictitious, and any
resemblance to real people, or events, is purely coincidental.

All rights reserved, including the right to reproduce this book,
or portions thereof, in any form.

The right of Storm Constantine to be identified as the author of
this work has been asserted by her in accordance with the
Copyright, Design and Patents Act, 1988.

http://www.stormconstantine.com

Cover: Ruby
Interior Illustrations: Olga Ulanova
Interior Design: Storm Constantine

Set in Book Antiqua

MB0149

ISBN 978-1-905713-55-4

A Megalithica Books edition
An imprint of Immanion Press Edition
http://www.immanion-press.com
info@immanion-press.com

Dedication

This book is dedicated to the memory of my father, John Martin Bristow. Thanks Dad, for making me aware of magic and wonder.

Preface

I wrote the first Wraeththu novels in the 1980s, but after the millennium returned to their world for a new series of books. The stories have always been inspired by vivid dreams, which I've had virtually all my life. My earliest Wraeththu tales were written in 1973.

Over the years, Wraeththu has attracted a loyal following of fans, many of whom empathised with, or were interested in, the magic of the novels. I thought it would be interesting to expand the ideas within the novels and Wraeththu system of magic.

The creation of magical systems can properly be defined as Chaos Magic. This does not mean it involves the conjuring of dark primordial forces or that practitioners have to follow an alarmingly sloping left-hand path, as some people who know nothing about it believe. Chaos Magic (or Pop Culture Magic) can be seen as working with the 'stuff' of creation, channelling new thought-forms, gods, rituals and practices. The Chaoticists perceive the possibility of magic in every walk of life and acknowledge the fact that icons of our culture can be viewed and used as magical entities.

The first thing required in a magical system is the focus – the entities of deities around which the system revolves. The gods of Wraeththu are called dehara (day-hara), singular dehar (day-har). They came to me as I was writing the fiction, presenting themselves to my imagination, often in astoundingly vivid forms, and are the foundation of this system of magic.

One of the ways in which this system was developed was through visionary questing, whereby the practitioner projects their mind into a visualised environment, then wanders through it, noting what they see and hear. This technique has been and is still used to quest for information about the Wraeththu gods, the dehara. Through this interaction, the system is as limitless as the imaginations of those involved in it. From a Chaos Magic point of view, practitioners are quite capable of creating new systems, thought forms and deities, which have as much relevance as existing systems, and are often more dynamic.

Gods and goddesses can be seen as thoughtforms or frequencies of the universal life force. The faces given to them are merely masks that enable people to interact with formless energy. Humans work better with pictures than abstract ideas. Also, when a great many people all invest energy – in the form of thought, intention and emotion – into something, it is fed by that energy and therefore acquires a kind of vicarious independent existence. What vitalises all the religions and magical systems of the world is: human thought, human emotion, human will and human intention.

The stuff of creation can be seen as a kind of modelling clay. It can be moulded into certain shapes, with certain attributes.

Although magic can be used to affect reality, in the form of rituals to achieve a desired effect, the individual practitioner can also use it as a tool for self-development. In the ancient system of alchemy, alchemists were said to be looking for the means to transform base metal into gold. While this might well have had a literal meaning, most people now accept that this was also a metaphor for spiritual enlightenment, the quest for true awareness and self-knowledge. The gold in question was that of the spirit, and all the different processes of the alchemical transformation applied to the being of the alchemist.

As for what people will get out of using this system, that is up to them. Like any magical tradition, it can be used to affect reality, in the form of majhahns (rituals) to achieve a specific effect, and to facilitate self-evolution through meditation and majhahn. I make no claims that Dehara is better than any other system; it is just different.

Another point I feel obliged to cover is that I am not, through this publishing this system, attempting to create a religion. To me, magic and religion are separate. This is magic. If used properly it can be a tool for self-progression, but that is down to the individual.

Five years after its first publication, I'm now reissuing Book One: Kaimana of the Grimoire Dehara in a paperback edition. I'm currently working on Book Two: Ulani, which I hope to publish within the next twelve months.

Thanks to everyone who has contributed to this project.

Introduction

The Wraeththu

In the novels, Wraeththu are a race of androgynous or hermaphrodite beings, (that is both male and female in one body), who come to replace humanity. A Wraeththu individual is called a 'har', and the plural of that word is 'hara'. They live in tribes and while some of them are nomadic, others occupy settlements, towns and cities. They are physically perfect beings, their bodies more efficient and resistant to disease than those of humans. They are more in tune with the environment, and are naturally adept at magical practices. Initially, hara were created from humans by a transformation process known as inception. Wraeththu blood has the capacity to mutate human DNA, so that a simple transfusion is all that's required to transform a human into a Wraeththu har. Eventually, in the stories, hara reproduce amongst themselves and as humanity dwindles there are fewer individuals to incept anyway. The gods with whom Wraeththu interact are created in their own image – as I believe is the case with human deities in the real world too. Wraeththu gods are called dehara, (singular: dehar).

The concept of the hermaphrodite has always been important in magical philosophy. It represents the union of opposites, true harmony of being. The word derives from the names of two Greek deities: the god Hermes and the goddess Aphrodite. I think it is an elegant term, but because it has acquired negative, almost sideshow, connotations, through earlier generations' misunderstanding of, and insensitivity to, people born with dual or unspecific gender, the word hermaphrodite is no longer a polite term to use in 'real life'. Magically, however, I think it's important to reclaim it as the spiritual symbol it is.

We live in a dualistic universe of opposites: male and female, light and dark, hot and cold and, of course, good and evil. The hermaphrodite symbolises the integration of these opposites. It is representative of DNA itself: the double helix, the twin serpent of the Caduceus wand, the Ouroboros snake of alchemy that bites its own tail. It combines the strengths of traditional male and female aspects; the passive and the active, the intuitive and the physical. In the Dehara system, practitioners visualise themselves as being androgynous in nature and the gods with whom they interact are also androgynous. By adopting this form, they step beyond the mundane limitations of the physical body.

As to what a har looks like, it should be seen as the perfect union of both genders, almost ethereal in appearance. Wraeththu do not have breasts (as they do not feed their young like humans do) or wide womanly hips, but neither are they bulging with muscles or 'triangular shaped' like the ideal of a male body. They are strong and agile, lean and fit.

While I usually refer to hara by the pronoun 'he', some people prefer a gender neutral pronoun instead. The least awkward of these is the singular pronoun set of 'they, them, their': i.e. 'ey', 'em', 'eir', etc.

Aruna or Sex Magic

Aruna: the exchange of essences. For Wraeththu, reproduction is just one aspect of physical communion. Its prime function for us is higher spiritual development. The har learns to refine its energy beyond mere pleasure. The hermaphrodite has long been regarded as a perfect archetype in many magical and religious systems. Humans struggled to understand and then strive spiritually for a concept that in us has become flesh. In alchemy, the androgyne is the rebus, the union of the alchemical king and queen, the fruit of the sacred marriage. In eastern systems, the balance of male and female principles was a desired quality: the harmony of yin and yang. We are a physical expression of the double helix, the entwined serpents. The feminine principle within us is called soume, and its organ is soume-lam. Magically, its main properties are coolness, moistness and passivity. The male principle is ouana, and its organ is ouana-lim. Its main magical properties are heat, dryness and activity. The generative organs are a microcosmic reflection of the main energy centres of the body. The har discovers the myriad uses to which these energies can be put during their training.

Thiede-har-Gelaming
'The Enchantments of Flesh and Spirit'

Sex between Wraeththu is termed aruna and is considered a spiritual practice. It is not simply a means for reproduction, but can be a majhahn that affects reality. It plays a big part in the novels, so cannot be ignored in the Deharan magical system. Androgynous sex is not something you can do in reality, but if you feel comfortable with the idea, you can visualise this activity in meditation. If you already have a sexual partner with whom you practice magic, then obviously you can experiment with the concept, but it is not an obligatory part of the system.

This system does not revolve purely around sex magic, because there are many other ways of interacting with universal energy, the Source, God, or whatever you want to call it. Sex magic is something that individuals can explore in their own way, if they feel so inclined. That said, many people who have worked with this system have reported they've 'taken aruna' with entities they've met in their visualisations, and that often knowledge has been imparted this way. The important thing to remember is to do only that with which you are comfortable. If you simply visualise yourself as a beautiful har during meditations, that is more than enough.

However, for those who wish to know more about aruna, here are the details. A har is both male and female and has all the required organs for this function. They can take a dominant or passive role in aruna, and do not have to stick to the same role. When visualising a harish partner, you can imagine them as an idealised version of yourself, the components of your male and female sides, your animus and anima. Aruna is not just about physical gratification. It is a spiritual practice, and a way to connect with the Source.

When Wraeththu reproduce, they create pearls, which are like eggs. The pearl is dropped by the hostling and then gives forth a couple of weeks later. This concept is incorporated into the seasonal festivals, known as arojhahns, which is part of the Neoma level.

Inception

Hara become Aralids, (studying the first tier of the system), once they are incepted, i.e. once their human form is transformed. The ceremony in which this takes place is called Harhune. The early level of Dehara incorporates a Harhune visualisation, during which the practitioner creates for

14

themselves an androgynous form for Dehara majhahns (rituals).

The Magical Caste System

Dehara follows the Wraeththu magical caste system. Caste in this case does not apply to rigid social status, but nine levels of three tiers through which the student, or rehuna, progresses. Although this book concentrates solely upon the Kaimana tier, the whole list of levels is given below. Further books will focus on the other two tiers.

The nine levels are crowned by a level beyond corporeal existence, equating with Aghama, or divinity.

To pronounce these names, stress the syllables typed in bold.

KAIMANA (**Ky**-ee-**mar**-nah) 'The Path of the Seeker'

1: Ara - altar (**Ar**-ah)
2: Neoma - new moon (Nee-**oh**-mah)
3: Brynie – strong (**Bry**-nee)

ULANI (Oo-**lar**-nee) 'The Path of the Cosmos'

1: Acantha - thorny (A-**canth**-uh)
2: Pyralis – fire (py-**ral**-iss)
3: Algoma - valley of flowers (al-**goh**-mah)

NAHIR-NURI (Na-**heer** Noo-**ree**) 'The Path of the Infinite'

1: Efrata – distinguished (Eff-**rah**-tuh)
2: Aislinn - vision (**Ayz**-linn)
3: Cleatha - glory (Clee-**ah**-thuh)

Rehunas of Kaimana and Ulani are known by their level, i.e., an individual of Acantha level would be known as Acanthalid.

Ara – aralid
Neoma – neomalid
Brynie – brynilid
Acantha – acanthalid
Pyralis – Pyralisit
Algoma – algomalid

Once Nahir-Nuri has been achieved, however, the caste divisions are no longer used as a title of address. Rehunas of that caste are simply called Nahir-Nuri.

Symbols and Sigils

In Kaimana, there are three symbols associated with the different levels: Ara, Neoma and Brynie. They have been 'programmed', (through the will and intention of those developing this system), to control energy invoked or created during the workings. For example, the symbol Ara is drawn to represent a portal to the imaginary realms. To close that portal, the symbol is drawn in reverse.

There are also different symbols for each dehar, for certain etheric locations, as well as for various aspects of the dehara. All of the symbols and sigils in the grimoire were received during meditations.

Majhahn Tools

The implement used during invocations and to direct energy during majhahn is referred to as the vakei. In the absence of this tool, the practitioner uses the first two fingers of their dominant hand to direct energy.

For some of the workings, practitioners can use shayyai, which are flame proof bowls of methylated spirits set alight.

Other substances can be burned, such as ghee (clarified butter), in which case a wick will also be required.

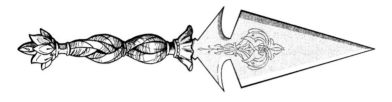

Agmara Energy

All matter is made up of energy. At the microcosmic level, objects do not exist in the same way they are perceived by human senses. If people had the ability to perceive the particles of which things are made up, rather than just the human wider view of solid objects, it might be difficult to discern the boundaries between 'things'. In essence, all things would be linked, blending into one another. Energy is life. It is creation itself. It is what things are made of and is also the 'glue' that holds them together.

Practitioners of magic have access to this energy as a continual and limitless power source for their workings. It can help affect changes in the environment or be used for self development. It is healing and promotes self awareness.

Humans are part of this force, forever connected to it, born from it, returned to it. Whether we retain any form of consciousness beyond physical earthly incarnation is a subject that only the individual can make their minds up about, since there is no hard evidence about it. But few would argue that once we die, the energy of our physical form doesn't (indeed can't) just disappear. Energy can only change form, absorbed back into the source. This boundless fount of energy is referred to as 'agmara' in the Dehara system. The name derives from the Wraeththu progenitor and demi-god Aghama. It is the primary power source.

Basic Magical Principles and Techniques

At the back of the Grimoire, there are appendices that provide basic information about breathing exercises, meditation and visualisation, to which new practitioners can refer

.

Ara

The Path of the Aralid

Come walk with me upon the path that leads between the stars...

Kaimana is the first tier. It is the outer court of dehara. Its name means 'the path of the seeker'.

Ara is the first level of Kaimana. Aralid is the student. Ara is the approach to and understanding of agmara. Agmara is the life force of the universe, which is within everything. The dehara are part of this energy. It constitutes their form.

The tools of the Aralid are the breath and the mind. Ara is inception, the gateway to the inner realms of the imagination. Inception is virtual transformation. The name of this ceremony is Harhune.

Harhune is the first majhahn, (mazh-**arn**), a magical procedure or ritual. It is conducted by a hienama (**hy**-en-ah-muh), a shaman concerned with inception, initiation and magical training.

Practitioners of Dehara are known as rehunas (sing. rehuna: reh-**hoo**-nah). This is the term for both seeker and priest – one who studies the unseen and who might officiate at majhahns when a hienama's services are not required. All those who have studied to Brynie level have enough knowledge to lead

21

Deharan majhahns. Hienamas are required to have trained to third level Ulani – Algoma.

The term for a group of rehunas practicing together is ruhahn (roo-**harn**). The plural term for such groups is ruhahna.

Harhune

Light flared up ahead of me and the dark rafters of the Nayati loomed above, suddenly visible, encrusted with gargoyle faces that laughed and screamed forever in silence. Tall metal stands formed an avenue before me. They supported filigree bowls of incense that exuded smoke so heavy it drifted downwards in matted shrouds.

At the far end of the hall, in the wing opposite, I caught sight of a white table that gleamed like marble. And beyond that?

A slim reed of light opened out like a flower. Tall. Dressed in white. A halo of fiery, red-gold hair. An angel. A demon. The Hienama.

Pellaz-har-Aralis
'The Enchantments of Flesh and Spirit'

The rehuna composes themselves in their majhahn space. When the body and mind is sufficiently relaxed, it is imagined that the environment is disappearing into a grey mist. The rehuna takes themselves, as a spark of consciousness, into an empty void.

The mist begins to clear away before the inner eye, and as it does so, the rehuna becomes aware of sound before seeing anything. The roar of voices is heard; it is as if the rehuna is waking from a dream to a new and concrete reality.

The rehuna finds themselves in a Nayati, which is a Wraeththu sacred place or temple. It may be a building or a site outdoors. The rehuna has been brought to this place for inception. Around them, hara have gathered to witness the process. They are chanting the word 'Harhune!'

The rehuna should centre themselves in this reality. They are taking part in a rite of passage. Their whole being is about to change. They should experience to the full the emotions and thoughts this process evoke in them. The har who will incept them is called a hienama. He is a har of at least Algoma level. He comes forward now to lead the rehuna to the altar. He is visualised as the rehuna wills: a beautiful and benevolent being.

The rehuna then visualises that the hienama cuts their flesh and transfuses blood into them. He makes a wound in his own flesh, and presses this to their own. The rehuna feels his essence going into them, changing their being, making them stronger, more aware, more alive. They should sense that they are transforming into an androgyne, a form they will use for their Dehara majhahns. It is a body they will reserve in their imagination for interaction with the dehara. It is a magical tool, like a robe.

The rehuna should be conscious of their harish body – its male and female aspects, beyond mere surface gender attributes. They should be comfortable in this condition. They should think about the psychological implications, how being utterly balanced might feel. It is important for the rehuna not to feel this as any kind of diminishing, but rather a perfect ideal state, something beyond this mundane world. They should think about how male and female sometimes feel like entirely different species, unable to communicate properly, and contemplate what it would be like to be free of this dichotomy, to fully understand how each other thinks and feels.

The hienama tells the rehuna that in order to achieve evolution, of any kind, they must be free of illusion, free of mundane cares, able to rise above the trivia of everyday life and view things from a higher perspective. In this place, they face themselves and their demons with no barrier. Once they have crossed the boundary, there is no going back. Awareness cannot be turned off. Once they have it, it is with them always, and sometimes that can be a painful and isolating condition. Worthwhile knowledge does not come easily.

> *Know yourself. Self knowledge is the hardest path of all,*
> *and any who tells you otherwise cannot possibly have it.*

The rehuna continues this visualisation for a few minutes, using the imagination. They may attend a gathering with others to celebrate the inception, or else take aruna with the hienama or another har to conclude the inception. They may seek their harish name, the one who will give it to them. The rehuna is free to take this visualisation in any direction they desire.

When the rehuna is ready to return to normal consciousness, they should visualise the scene before them fading away into a grey mist. They should be aware of the physical self in the real world, and cast off the visualised androgynous form. They should come back into themselves, as they really are. The mist begins to fade once more and the room they are sitting in reappears in the mind's eye. The rehuna should ground themselves by moving the fingers and toes. They should be conscious of the breath going in and out of the body. When they are ready, they should open their eyes.

The rehuna should record the results of the meditation, through words and pictures.

From now on, when the rehuna performs meditations, they should take on the visualised androgynous form at the beginning of each session. The rehuna may devise their own procedure for this, such as going to a particular place in the mind to adopt this form, or meeting with their hienama beforehand whose touch, gaze or words brings the androgynous form into being.

Agmara

Agmara is the breath of the universe. It is the rehuna's own breath. It is thought, emotion, the elements, the stuff of creation. The flesh of the dehara is wrought of agmara; it is their blood, their sinew, their essence.

Agmara is the force that works magic. It is the current between possibilities and possibility itself. Its colour is generally a radiant greenish white, but occasionally it might be visualised in different hues for particular purposes.

Agmara is moved with the will, which is part of it. When the rehuna summons agmara, they should feel its flood throughout their being. It is with them always but when the attention is turned elsewhere they do not feel it. Beneath the light of the rehuna's awareness, agmara grows stronger within them.

The Experience of Agmara

The rehuna composes themselves into a meditative state and transforms into the harish majhahn self.

The rehuna calls upon agmara:
'I call upon the mysterious ray of agmara. Be present here. Fill my being and this space around me.'

A ray of greenish-white energy is visualised, coming down from the centre of the universe. It enters the head through the crown chakra (a point just above the head) and travels down the body into the eviya. This area lies just behind the navel, and is where the rehuna visualises their personal life force or chi residing.

The rehuna should see their own life force as a white flame. The ray of agmara merges with it, vitalising and expanding it. This beneficial energy fills the body and radiate outwards from it. The rehuna should feel themselves being refreshed and renewed by it.

The rehuna should stay with this visualisation for a few minutes, breathing deeply. Concentration should be applied to linking with agmara, to feeling it. The rehuna should note any physical sensations they might experience.

When the rehuna is ready to conclude the meditation, they should ground themselves by placing both hands against the eviya. The palms of the hands might seem quite hot. The rehuna should breathe deeply for some moments. They should centre themselves in their actual physical form, casting off the androgynous visualised self. They should imagine their surroundings in the physical world, and move the fingers and toes. When the rehuna is ready, they should open their eyes.

The Symbol Ara

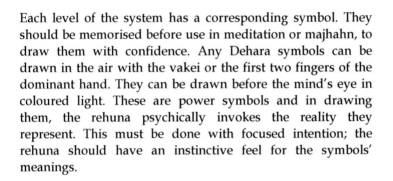

Each level of the system has a corresponding symbol. They should be memorised before use in meditation or majhahn, to draw them with confidence. Any Dehara symbols can be drawn in the air with the vakei or the first two fingers of the dominant hand. They can be drawn before the mind's eye in coloured light. These are power symbols and in drawing them, the rehuna psychically invokes the reality they represent. This must be done with focused intention; the rehuna should have an instinctive feel for the symbols' meanings.

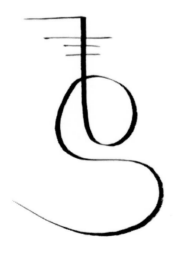

Whenever a symbol is drawn, its name may be spoken three times. The name of the symbol is its mantra. The name can be chanted in majhahn. The symbol can be drawn or painted onto the body.

Ara symbolises the gateway into other realms. It is the fundamental symbol of Dehara and its colour as light is white. It summons energy and opens doors. It is used at the beginning of majhahns to open a portal to other realities. It is also used when channelling agmara to focus the energy frequency to the relevant purpose.

Ara is drawn by beginning at the top left, then adding the three horizontal lines.

Because it creates portals, Ara should initially be used with care. To begin working with it, the rehuna should first memorise it thoroughly by drawing it and visualising it, so that it can be imagined easily by the mind's eye. The rehuna should learn also to draw it in reverse.

When the rehuna is familiar with the symbol, they should meditate upon it. The symbol should be drawn in the air before them, (imagined as comprised of white light), or in their mind, saying the name three times. While the rehuna is meditating, visualised images may come to them, which should be recorded in some manner thereafter.

To conclude the meditation on Ara, it is drawn in reverse, either in the air or in the mind. This closes the gateway. This should be visualised clearly as the symbol is drawn.

Ara and Agmara

Once the rehuna has meditated for some time on both agmara and Ara, they should combine the two. They should call upon agmara and draw the symbol Ara. It is visualised that the symbol facilitates the flow of agmara and allows the rehuna to experience it more fully. The meditation is concluded by drawing Ara in reverse and placing the hands upon the eviya.

Agmara Healing

> *I cleaned the wound and placed my hands above it to project the healing frequency of agmara. I augmented the healing with a visualisation of the crushed bone knitting back together. I would get a sense of the energy taking effect, a focussing of agmara within me....*
>
> **Pellaz-har-Aralis**
> **'The Enchantments of Flesh and Spirit'**

Agmara may also be used to facilitate healing.

The rehuna performs the usual agmara/Ara meditation and calls upon agmara to flow through them. It is visualised that the energy enters the body and fills it, then leaves it through the hands and feet.

This energy may be directed into recipient, by either placing the hands gently on or near them. Agmara should be visualised streaming from the hands as a healing force and entering the recipient. The rehuna should relax into this procedure. They should also resist putting personal energy into the process. They should visualise that the energy comes from outside of them, from the source of creation. It does not deplete or tire them to channel it.

The procedure is ended by placing the hands on the eviya to ground the energy.

Self Knowledge

> *Intelligence welled within me, as my situation hardened into sharp focus in my brain. I was so earthbound, so wrapped up in myself, blind to essential truths. Emotion filled me. The truth about everything, the universe itself, was within my grasp. The door was opening to me...*
>
> **Pellaz-har-Aralis**
> **'The Enchantments of Flesh and Spirit'**

One of the most important concepts within the study of Dehara is that of knowing yourself. It is a life long lesson that should be practiced regardless of whether the rehuna is a novice or an experienced practitioner. Even if they have practiced for many years, they constantly have experiences that evolve and change them. The rehuna should observe themselves from an impartial and distanced position, to see how these experiences contribute to any difficulties in their life or help them develop as an individual.

Knowledge of the self is not the easiest path. Sometimes, the seeker faces fears and inner conflicts they would rather avoid. But the key to practicing *bona fide* majhahn is to face fears and recognise them for what they are. This makes the rehuna stronger and more whole; unexpected bubbles from the dark swamp of the psyche are less likely to catch them unawares.

As an Aralid, the rehuna should develop the capacity to observe themselves without judgement. They should chart their habitual behaviours and strategies. Which ones are most effective? Which ones do not work? They should ask themselves the basic yet fundamental questions: who am I? What do I want? What am I afraid of and why?

The rehuna should take responsibility for their own life. They should not seek to blame others for their misfortunes.

> *A student of the great Kakkahaar magus, Velisarius, once said, 'Tiahaar, you tell me I am the owner of all my feelings and reactions, yet isn't it natural to be angry if an enemy offends me? I did not ask him to offend me, yet he does. In essence, he put the anger into me with his actions.'*
>
> *Velisarius considered these words and then took his student to a place where three hara were sitting around a fire. 'Go up to them,' Velisarius said, 'and tell them you have received a message from the ethers. Tell them that they are a disgrace to their tribe, and that their decadent and indolent ways disgust you.'*
>
> *The student was naturally hesitant. 'Are they really these things?'*
>
> *'That is irrelevant,' Velisarius replied. 'Do as I say.'*

So the student approached the group and made his announcement. For some moments, they stared at him in surprise, then one of them laughed. Another put his hands against his mouth, his eyes showing his fear. The third stood up, raised his fist and knocked the student to the floor.

The student went back to his teacher, rubbing his face. 'What am I to learn form that, tiahaar, other than it is best not insult others unless I want to get hurt?'

'Surely, it is very simple,' Velisarius said. 'All three heard the same words from your lips, and each one reacted differently to them. Did you put those reactions into those hara?'

The student pondered this. 'No,' he said at last. 'They reacted individually.'

'Exactly,' said Velisarius. 'In any situation, confronted by any stimulus, you choose how to react, and the reaction belongs to you alone. Be mindful of this in all areas of life. Do not react without awareness. Be still for a moment before you act or react.' He smiled. 'Perhaps now you should apologise. The same experiment applies. I would suggest you be prepared to duck another blow.'

Lianvis-har-Kakkahaar

The Hienama

During the inception meditation, the rehuna meets a hienama who transforms them. This being is their spiritual teacher in the world of Dehara. He is both part of themselves and an entity in his own right. He belongs to them. The more the rehuna communes with him in meditation, the stronger he will appear as a personality. His character is built up by interaction with him. As well as performing the agmara and Ara meditations, part of the work in this level is to develop the hienama. The rehuna creates this magical entity to work with them.

The rehuna should visualise meetings with their hienama. They should discover his name and his history. They should build up details about him. The hienama may be asked to help the rehuna in various ways, either by imparting information or supplying support, in the form of strength or confidence. Sometimes, details might come through as inspired information. At other times, the rehuna might impose their own preferences on the hienama, such as the way he looks, speaks or is dressed. The manner in which he is created is irrelevant. He comes from the mind in either case. He should be designed so that the rehuna feels secure with him. If, for any reason, some part of a visualisation or majhahn should unnerve, the rehuna may call upon the hienama to be with them and protect them. He should be created to have a great deal of experience and expertise, even beyond what the rehuna can imagine.

The rehuna should ask the hienama to take them on visualised journeys and to give them lessons. The rehuna should show him more about their world; friends, family and environment. The rehuna should interact with him in respect of learning about themselves. He is part of their inner world, a created entity, who they can programme to access the farthest corners of their mind.

The Nayati

The rehuna will create their own Nayati, which they visualise each time they meditate. They can begin every visualisation by imagining this place. A Nayati can be a building or a sacred site outdoors. It should be designed according to personal preference, with detail added as time goes on. A visualised temple is often known by the term 'inner plane temple'. The inner plane refers to the astral realm, the realm beyond mundane reality, the spiritual realm, a realm of pure energy. In Dehara, it is referred to as 'the ethers'. The 'etheric

Nayati' refers to that of the inner plane, while plain 'Nayati' refers to majhahn space in reality.

The rehuna should create a sigil to act as a gateway to their Nayati. It can be used for protection while in meditation.

Neoma

The Path of the Neomalid

In Ara, the lessons were Harhune, connection with agmara, knowledge of the first symbol, and the concept of self-knowledge. In Neoma the rehuna begins to interact with the dehara themselves.

Neoma also includes the Dehara seasonal cycle, and the arojhahns for the solstices, equinoxes and cross quarter days.

The Symbol Neoma

The first task of the second level Kaimana is to become familiar with the symbol Neoma, which represents a shield of protection. In majhahn, it is used once the gate has been opened by Ara to safeguard against 'fallout' or negative energy experiences. Its colour is purple.

It can be used in any situation, in conjunction with agmara, to promote security, well-being and protection against stray energy. In meditation, the rehuna opens up to whatever energy is present in the environment, and perhaps also to whatever other rehunas in the world of

Dehara have been doing – all are interconnected when they access this realm. Neoma acts as a screen against potential negative energy.

Neoma is drawn by beginning at the top left. The two lines are added after the main body of the symbol. As with Ara, the rehuna should practice meditating on the symbol and become familiar with it. It's not necessary for them to learn how to draw it in reverse.

Once the rehuna knows it well, they should perform the agmara meditation, using both Ara and Neoma symbols at the start. Now they can progress further into the inner realms, and Neoma protects them as you travel.

The meditation is concluded by drawing Ara in reverse and placing the hands upon the eviya.

Neoma Initiation

To formalise this level, the rehuna should perform an initiation visualisation similar to the Harhune meditation they undertook in Ara.

The rehuna should compose themselves for meditation, summon agmara to flow through them, and assume the harish self.

The etheric Nayati is visualised forming around them.

At this level, the initiation is less of a public spectacle. Only the hienama and some of his higher level students are present. The Nayati is solemn and dark. The majhahn takes place at night.

The meditation is invested with as much personal imagery as possible.

The hienama raises the rehuna's caste level by directing agmara energy into their body at a higher vibration. This can be done in several ways. In a simple 'attunement' of energy, the hienama draws Ara and Neoma in air, or upon the rehuna's body, invests the symbols with power, and directs them into the rehuna's eviya. This can be through the breath, the gaze or channelling with the hands. Alternatively, (or additionally), he may take aruna with the rehuna for the same purpose. Whatever method is chosen to visualise, the rehuna should concentrate on feeling a stronger pulse of agmara within them. They should be aware that their ability to work with it is strengthened.

After the ceremony, the rehuna should commune with the hienama for as long as they wish and return to mundane reality when they are ready to do so.

When the rehuna has concluded the meditation, they should celebrate in some way. If they work in ruhahn, all present should of a feast.

The Dehara

Dehara are formed from agmara itself. There are five main dehara: Aruhani, Miyacala, Agave, Lunil and Aghama. Seasonal, elemental and purpose-built entities are known as dehara vegrandis. Temporary entities, or beings fashioned for a specific limited purpose, are known as dehara demitto.

Neoma concentrates on the five main dehara and the seasonal dehara vegrandis.

Each of the five dehara is represented by a coloured flame, which reflects his frequency of energy. The names are pronounced by putting the stress on the syllables in bold type.

Aghama (**Ag**-uh-mah)

> *Wraeththu speak of the Aghama sometimes, not as often as they should, bearing in mind what he should mean to them, but when they do, it is in veiled terms of his still being involved in manipulating our race. A misty figure: part god, part monster. They are not wrong.*
>
> **Pellaz-har-Aralis**
> **'The Enchantments of Flesh and Spirit'**

This is the sign of the Aghama, creator of Wraeththu, the first har and dehar of all. Its colour is the rainbow spectrum. Unlike the other dehara, the Aghama represents an incarnate individual as well as a spiritual entity. He is the embodiment of agmara. His fleshly form is Thiede, a har of intense almost terrifying beauty, who usually has flame-red hair. His etheric form is a

41

more ethereal version of this image. Aghama corresponds to the fifth element of spirit. He is called into the centre of the Nayati. His flame is rainbow-coloured, representing all frequencies. Cabbalistically, he corresponds to Kether, the highest sphere. His epithets include: Lord of the Cosmos, Tigron of the Spheres and Avatar of Beauty.

 Samuntala, the etheric Nayati of the Aghama, is a vast complex, containing within its labyrinthine courts a multitude of shrines to other dehara, some of whom have yet to be formed. The spiritual beliefs of every culture in creation can be glimpsed in the Nayati's design. The rehuna might pass from a colonnaded walkway lined by sphinxes into the courtyard of a majestic pagoda. Some areas are completely alien, as if mirroring the architecture of some far world beyond the imagination. This is its sign.

In order to enter Samuntala, the rehuna draws the symbols of Aghama and his Nayati upon the air. A portal to it is visualised opening in the centre of the majhahn space in reality. The rehuna rises up from their body and enters this doorway.

The Aghama is a benevolent presence, although his other aspect Thiede can be a trickster. Aghama is approached for matters of protection and fortune. He also bestows inspiration, creativity and adaptability. The solution to problems and dilemmas can be sought in his Nayati.

Aruhani (A-roo-**har**-nee)

Flick lit a fire and stood before it. He wore only, wrapped around his loins, the skin of a coyote. He loosed his hair and held his arms to the sky. Now, he must do it. Now, he must believe. He would call upon one of the deities he had named. In his mind, he saw Aruhani, his braided hair like snakes. This was not a comfortable image, for Aruhani was capricious and sometimes sly. But he was the dehar of life, aruna and death, so the most appropriate in this instance. Flick concentrated on the image in his head. He tried to feel the deity as well as see him. He took a deep breath and called, 'Aruhani, I call you! Come to me now, in the name of the Aghama, the principle of creation! I command you! I bring blood as an offering. Hear me and approach!

From 'The Wraiths of Will and Pleasure'

 This is the sign of the dehar Aruhani, who is known also as the Devourer, the Hostling of Bones, The Beautiful One, He Whose Body is the Sky. The colour of the symbol is black with gold sparks within it. Aruhani presides over aruna, life and death. He is a protective and creative principle as well as an unpredictable destructive one. His skin is black, and his dark hair is worn in many braids that cover him like a shawl. His face, arms and chest may be decorated with swirling patterns in red pigment. He is the most capricious of the dehara and yet the most compassionate. The most mystic of his representations is when he is shown displaying his soume-lam, but with an erect ouana-lim also. Aruhani is perhaps the strongest and most

43

fearsome of the dehara. Cabbalistically, he combines aspects of Netzach and Binah. His is the black flame of destruction and creation. His direction is north.

The etheric Nayati of Aruhani is Julangis and here is its sign:

Julangis is situated on a strange alien world, where the light is golden yellow, yet the landscape black and rocky. There are many glassy lakes with gilded surfaces and strange trees of peculiar hues. To enter the Nayati, the rehuna proceeds to a huge stepped pyramid, which is climbed. The entrance to Julangis is at the apex of the pyramid. Aruhani's inner shrine lies beneath this structure. Even though it is apparently deep beneath the ground, it feels open to the sky. It is a jungle garden with an altar in its centre. Aruhani manifests sitting upon this altar.

Although formidable, Aruhani makes a strong and fiercely protective ally. He can be approached concerning any problem or lack in life. He promotes physical and material comfort, and is also a shielding dehar of the young. He also bestows fertility, should it be desired. The sign of Aruhani is a protective talisman that can be worn in jewellery or permanently as a tattoo. The sign invokes him in his benevolent form, but even this aspect can be petitioned to right wrongs and to take decisive or destructive action. The Devourer is his aspect as the uncontrollable forces of nature, before which all living beings are defenceless. As the Hostling of Bones, Aruhani sits at the base of Tree of Life, known in Dehara as Dryalimah. In this aspect, approach him to drink of the Waters of Forgetfulness or the Waters of Remembrance.

Miyacala (My-uh-car-lah)

The dehara came to Flick at any time of day or night. He would be walking in the hills, and a name would come to him. One time, as he watched a flight of birds erupt from the canopy of trees and spiral, screeching, into the sky, he heard in his mind the name Miyacala, and an image came to him of a tall, white-haired har, whose eyes were milky blind, but whose forehead burned with a silver star. Flick knew then that Miyacala needed no physical eyes to see, for his sight was of the psychic kind. He was a dehar of initiation and magic, and those hara who studied and honed their skills walked in the prints of his sacred feet.

From 'The Wraiths of Will and Pleasure'

Here is the sign of the dehar Miyacala, who presides over initiation (inception) and the intellectual and practical aspects of magical work. Its colour is sparkling white. Among Miyacala's epithets are Lord of the Libraries of the Cosmos and Walker Upon the North Star Road. He appears dressed in white, with long white hair, and his eyes are milky blind. He has a star on his forehead, which represents his true inner sight and when he raises his left hand, there is a star of light there also. He grants caste ascension through the light of his left hand, which comes directly from the Source. Cabbalistically, he channels Kether, so belongs in the sephiroth Chokmah. His is the pure white flame of knowledge. His direction is east.

The Nayati of Miyacala is Tahanica, and its sign is below.

Tahanica's main chamber is long and lined by tall white columns. At the end of the chamber, a flight of white stairs leads to a dais that contains the altar, which is a cube of marble. There is a tall tripod here also, upon which burns an eternal flame of searing white light.

Miyacala is approached for mental creativity, for inspiration, knowledge, magical progression, and initiation. He can also issue wise judgements in matters of difficult choice. His light brings truth, and can strip away delusion, falsehoods and deceit. In his presence, liars are unmasked or betray themselves. He brings justice in cases of slander and libel.

Agave (A-gar-vay)

Accidentally brushing against the blade of a leaf caused a painful cut. Flick told Lileem there was strong magic in the plant and she said that perhaps there was a dehar of agave, who was a dehar of weapons, pain and war. 'That is his name, of course,' she said. 'Agave. Perhaps we should make him an offering and say a prayer.'

Lileem described Agave and his preferences in terms of offerings, then said gravely, 'Flick has seen the dehara, the gods. We see them together now. They are pouring out of the stars.'

From 'The Wraiths of Will and Pleasure'

The sign of Agave, dehar of flame and fiery will, is blood red with crimson sparks within it. Agave is named for the agave plant of the Sierra Madre, which can cause terrible injuries with its razor sharp leaves. In one aspect he appears as

 dressed in strange organic armour, almost like an insect carapace, which when removed reveals him as a golden creature of sun and flame. He is a Shaman warrior but also a healer. His hair is a brilliant red, the colour of blood. His eyes are the colour of orange flames and his skin pigment is a mixture of orange, red, and yellow. When he speaks, his voice is the crackling of flames. In his right hand, he holds a spear, which symbolizes his masculinity. In his left hand, he holds a shield, which symbolizes his femininity. He is called, among other things, The Warrior of Eternal Fire and Walker of Battlefields.

As a protector, when invoked, Agave stands by the shoulder of the rehuna. He may appear wreathed in flames; a bold presence. His flames burn destructively in this form, and can be used to burn an individual or situation from the rehuna's life. As a healer, Agave is gentle. In healing situations, the rehuna may invoke Agave and ask for his curative flame to augment agmara.

Agave values honesty, particularly honesty with those who would work with him. He is the red flame of passion. Cabbalistically, his qualities embody both Geburah (for his warlike aspect) and Tiphareth (for solar aspect). His direction is south. The Nayati of Agave is Igniteran, and its sign is: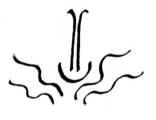

Igniteran is located in an arid landscape of high forbidding cliffs of orange rock. Its entrance is at the mouth of a cave, and is decorated with tall columns and carvings of deharan spirits. Within, are many chambers leading deep into the cliffs. In some eternal flames burn, while in the deepest areas are deep pits that connect with the hot core of the world. Igniteran is a dark and smouldering place, with shadowy hienamas gliding through its chambers, but it is not a place to inspire dread. Within its precincts, a visiting rehuna can call upon the strength and fire of Agave; they can be healed or learn some of the dehar's secrets. Agave is found in the deepest chamber, where he sits enthroned upon a golden chair.

In his warrior aspect, Agave is approached to resolve matters of hostility expediently. In his healing aspect, he can ameliorate dysfunctions of the body, as well as destructive situations. He strengthens the will of the rehuna and refines occult techniques. He bestows energy and brings warmth to cold places, whether in the heart or the environment. In circumstances where the rehuna requires protection, Agave may be invoked to stand at the rehuna's shoulder, for as long as needed. He can similarly be sent to protect others.

Lunil (Loo-nil)

'Lunil keeps a bird with silver feathers who has three heads. One speaks only the truth, another only lies, while the third speaks in riddles.'

She insisted that one night, she had seen Lunil with her own eyes. He had flown out of the moon as a flock of ghostly owls, only to transform into a silver skinned har with blue hair, who had danced in the tree outside her bedroom window and sung to her.

From 'The Wraiths of Will and Pleasure'

This is the sign of Lunil, the dehar associated particularly with the moon and lunar qualities. Its colour is a brilliant sparkling sapphire. Lunil is the dehar of the blue flame, a cold radiance that represents the immortal fire that burned on ancient altars, the fire of eternal life. Lunil might occasionally manifest a fey

51

fragile quality, but has also a far stronger aspect, as potent as fiery Agave. Lunil and Agave work well together: the red hot flame of passion and the cool blue flame of psychic ability. Lunil is visualised as having blue skin and hair. His eyes emanate either a smoking azure light or a vibrant violet. When invoked he often appears naked, or may be clothed in diaphanous veils of light. He embodies watery and lunar attributes: psychism, divination, and the emotional drive behind majhahn. On the Cabbalistic Tree of Life, he would be found in Yesod. His direction is west. Among his epithets are the title Hienama of the Spheres and Guardian of the Inner Ways.

The Nayati of Lunil is Loraylah, and its sign is:

Loraylah is a shining edifice of shifting elements; its chambers have a wavering, nebulous quality. Throughout the Nayati are fountains and cascades of blue, silver and violet light. In the inner sanctum, Lunil sits enthroned. The chamber is domed and streams of luminous fluid flow down its walls. The floor is a shallow radiant pool but for a walkway that leads to the dais of the throne. There is no altar here.

Lunil is approached to strengthen intuitive faculties, to give insight into nebulous situations, to refine emotions, and to assist in matters of the heart. He can mitigate tumultuous situations and calm hysteria and anger. He can also purge the rehuna of negative or painful emotions. Because he also represents the veils of the Moon, he can be used to conceal things, to keep them safely hidden. As a teacher, he is inspirational and can be invoked to stand at the rehuna's side during creative projects, enabling the flow of ideas.

Meditating on the Dehara

The rehuna should perform their usual agmara meditation, using both Ara and Neoma. Once in a meditative state, they should visualise one of the dehara. The rehuna should familiarise themselves with each dehar in turn, imagining them in the mind's eye. At this stage, the rehuna should concentrate on visualising their images rather than initiating communication. This is the first stage of forming a connection with the dehara. If some form of interaction should happen spontaneously, the rehuna should allow the experience to unfold as it will, and record their experience afterwards.

After each meditation, if the rehuna is artistically inclined, they can draw or paint the dehara as they imagined them. Should additional details come to the rehuna, they should add them to their personal image of the dehar. Each dehar is slightly different for each rehuna who visits them.

Nayati Building

The rehuna may create a Nayati in the physical space where majhahns take place. This Nayati will exist both in the inner and outer realms, creating a link between them. The creation of a Nayati in this sense is not mandatory, and subject to the personal choices and preferences of the rehuna. It is possible to work Deharan majhahns through visualisation in the etheric realms alone.

A room or outdoor location is transformed into a Nayati by the placement of majhahn objects, such as candles and an altar, in specific positions. The rehuna may direct agmara through the hands to charge up the energy of the environment, linking it to the etheric Nayati.

Candles in the colours of the dehara may be placed at each direction point. The altar may stand at any point of the rehuna's choosing; in one of the quarter areas or in the centre of the Nayati. The rehuna may burn incense or scented oil upon the altar.

Shayyai may be placed upon the altar or in the quarter areas. In some majhahns, shayyai may provide the only source of light. When they expire, the Nayati is in darkness. This is conducive to creating the desired atmosphere during majhahns of particular importance and gravity.

Dehara Quest Meditation

The rehuna may perform this meditation alone or with others.

It's preferable that the directional invocations are learned beforehand, rather than read from a script. A rehuna who is reading can't put as much intention into the proceedings as when the invocations are memorised.

In ruhahn, the invocations may be divided between several individuals. Alternatively, one rehuna can conduct the whole process.

The room is prepared for majhahn in the accustomed way. Appropriate music may be played. Candles and incense may be lit.

A rehuna stands in the centre of the room, and calls upon agmara energy.

'I call upon the mysterious ray of agmara, in all of its power and brilliance, to descend now from the centre of creation, to fill my being and transform this space into a sacred Nayati.'

The rehuna visualises that the radiance of agmara enters their body through the crown of the head and leaves it through the hands. For a few minutes, the rehuna holds up the hands, fingers splayed, to direct this energy into the environment. They visualise that everything around them becomes tinged with its light.

The rehuna draws Ara and Neoma in the air, in the centre of the room with the vakei or the first two fingers of the dominant hand. Ara is the gateway, and Neoma the shield. The symbols should be drawn large, using sweeps of the arm.

As Ara is drawn, the rehuna commands: 'Ara: you are the gateway.'

As Neoma is drawn, the rehuna commands: 'Neoma: you are the shield of protection'

Dehara Invocation

The rehuna should speak clearly, and visualise the dehar at each quarter as they invoke him. For ruhahn, the invocations may be changed to include plural personal pronouns rather than singular.

The rehuna goes to the north, draws the sign of Aruhani upon the air, raises arms and commands:

> *In this quarter, I call upon the dehar Aruhani,*
> *who stands in the North.*
> *Aruhani, dehar of aruna, life and death,*
> *Devourer and Creator,*
> *Be present in this Nayati*
> *Cast over me your gaze of smoking midnight*
> *Give me your strength and power*
> *In the name of the fifth element,*
> *Aghama, the star and your master.*

The rehuna draws the symbol Ara in the air, bows to Aruhani and visualises he bows to them also.

The rehuna goes to the east, draws the sign of Miyacala upon the air, raises arms, and commands:

> *In this quarter, I call upon the dehar Miyacala,*
> *who stands in the East*
> *Miyacala, dehar of initiation and knowledge*
> *Be present in this Nayati*
> *Cast over me the brilliance of your radiant eyes*
> *Give me your power of knowing*
> *In the name of the fifth element,*
> *Aghama, the star and your master.*

The rehuna draws the symbol Ara in the air, bows to Miyacala and visualises him bowing to them.

The rehuna goes to the south, draws the sign of Agave upon the air, raises arms, and commands:

> *In this quarter, I call upon the dehar Agave,*
> *who stands in the South*
> *Agave, dehar of fire in all its forms*
> *Be present in this Nayati*
> *Cast over me your sword of flame*
> *Give me your power of fiery will*
> *In the name of the fifth element,*
> *Aghama, the star and your master.*

The rehuna draws the symbol Ara in the air, bows to Agave and visualises him bowing to them.

The rehuna goes to the west, draws the sign of Lunil upon the air, raises arms, and commands:

> *In this quarter, I call upon the dehara Lunil,*
> *who stands in the West*
> *Lunil, dehar of lunar power and magic*
> *Be present in this Nayati*
> *Cast over me your cool blue flame*
> *Give me your power of insight and perception*
> *In the name of the fifth element,*
> *Aghama, the star and your master.*

The rehuna draws the symbol Ara in the air, bows to Lunil and visualises him bowing to them.

In the centre of the Nayati, the rehuna draws the sign of the Aghama upon the air, raises their arms and commands:

> *In the centre, I all call upon Aghama, Lord of the Cosmos,*
> *Tigron of the Spheres,*
> *Aghama, be present in this Nayati*
> *Protect and empower me!*

The rehuna bows to the Aghama, and visualises him bowing to them. (There is no requirement to draw Ara again.)

The Visualisation

The rehuna prepares as usual for majhahn.

Once the rehuna is fully relaxed, and has assumed the magical androgynous form, they should visualise the dehara in their quarters. The dehara are seen as standing in the portals to their realms. The rehuna's visualised self rises up from the physical body. In this form, the rehuna approaches the portal that calls to or attracts them the most.

The rehuna asks the dehar for permission to enter his realm. The rehuna may ask him to accompany them, or can pass through alone. Once through the portal, the rehuna should pause at the threshold to examine the landscape beyond it. When the rehuna is ready, they should walk into this landscape.

The rehuna should spend between 5-15 minutes exploring this realm, taking note of anything they see or hear. They might meet other beings or entities. Some rehunas find an amenable harish guide on their first visit, with whom they can work whenever they're meditating.

When the rehuna is ready to leave, they should conclude any

interaction with entities they might have encountered, and retrace their steps to the portal. The rehuna steps back through the portal, and acknowledged the dehar for his help and/or any information he has imparted. The rehuna visualises returning to the physical body and casting off the androgynous form. To re-establish contact with mundane reality, the rehuna should focus on their breathing as the air goes in and out of the chest, and should move the fingers and toes.

When the rehuna is ready, they open their eyes.

The rehuna should drink water, or whatever other refreshments are to hand, and relax for a while before dismantling the Nayati.

Dismantling the Nayati

It is important to close down the gateways between the imagined and the real world. When a rehuna addresses the dehara, they should do so in a commanding manner. When Ara is drawn in reverse, the rehuna should see the portal to the realm closing before them. The rehuna should focus on feeling that connection being severed. In each quarter, after the closing has been performed, mundane reality returns.

The rehuna goes to the north, raises arms, and commands:

> *'Aruhani, dehar of aruna, life and death*
> *Your presence here is always welcome.*
> *I release you from this Nayati*
> *Travel as you will*
> *In this world and all others,*
> *Until our paths cross again,*
> *In the name of the fifth element,*
> *Aghama, the star and your master,*
> *I bid you farewell.'*

Ara is drawn in reverse.

The rehuna goes to the east and commands:

Miyacala, dehar of initiation and knowledge,
Your presence here is always welcome.
I release you from this Nayati
Travel as you will
In this world and all others,
Until our paths cross again,
In the name of the fifth element,
Aghama, the star and your master,
I bid you farewell.

Ara is drawn in reverse

The rehuna goes to the south and commands:

Agave, dehar of fire,
Your presence here is always welcome.
I release you from this Nayati
Travel as you will
In this world and all others,
Until our paths cross again,
In the name of the fifth element,
Aghama, the star and your master,
I bid you farewell.

Ara is drawn in reverse

The rehuna goes to the west and commands:

Lunil, dehar of the moon and of magic,
Your presence here is always welcome.
I release you from this Nayati
Travel as you will
In this world and all others,
Until our paths cross again,
In the name of the fifth element,
Aghama, the star and your master,
I bid you farewell.

Ara is drawn in reverse

In the centre:

> 'Aghama, Child of the Cosmos,
> Your presence here is always welcome.
> I release you from this Nayati
> Travel as you will
> In this world and all others,
> Until our paths cross again,
> I bid you farewell.'

Ara is drawn, large, in the middle of the Nayati, in reverse.

Now the rehuna directs the agmara energy back to the centre of creation. It is imagined that the rehuna and the space they occupy become their usual mundane selves. Thus, the Nayati is dismantled.

The majhahn is now concluded.

The rehuna should record the results of their meditation as soon as possible, since details can be swiftly forgotten.

This meditation helps the rehuna lock on to the realms of the dehara. The more it is performed, so the more these realms and the dehara themselves will become alive for the rehuna. Details, physical characteristics, correspondences and attributes of the dehara will come through with increasing clarity. Entities the rehuna meets may become part of their majhahns.

Arotahar:
The Seasonal Cycle of Dehara

The arojhahns and images of the seasonal cycle represent the birth, death and rebirth of all life throughout the solar year. The name of this cycle is Arotahar; the endless rotation of the seasons, the planets, the moon and the sun. Majhahns celebrating Arotahar are known as arojhahns. Within the cycle, the dehar of Arotahar impregnates his son and then declines. His offspring then eventually gives forth a deharling that represents the infant sun, and the cycle is repeated. The name of the dehar is Panphilien, the lover of all. Every year, he is born, dies and is born again, giving himself in sacrifice to the land to ensure that life continues. He has twelve aspects, and is known by the names applied to him during his different reigns.

The theme of Arotahar is of hostling and son. For the first half of the year, they are together, and eventually become lovers, the dark dehar of winter transforming first into the joyous hostling of the winter solstice and later, the lover who impregnates the grown harling, who is destined to become in turn the dark dehar of Shadetide. At midsummer the dehar dies in the fields, leaving his lover/son alone through the dark months.

The Wheel of Arotohar

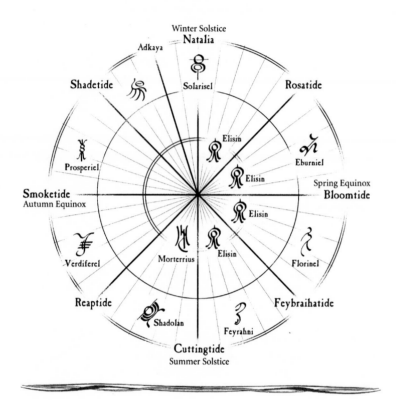

Natalia
December 21st

This is the arojhahn of the Winter Solstice, the longest night of the year. At this time, Elisin emerges from the pearl that nurtured him. The pearl was dropped two weeks previously, and now the deharling comes forth from it. He represents the reawakening of nature and the return of the sun. This is the new year of Dehara.

Solarisel, the deharling's hostling, is a benevolent dehar of great beauty, dressed in gold and white, with a mane of

64

golden hair. He grants the gift of a light heart, of fortune, promise and opportunity. He is the dehar of abundance, whose cauldron of creation offers up the ultimate potential. His is the arojhahn of the new sun. His plants are the holly, the ivy and the pine. He is accompanied by sleek white hounds, who at the moment of the deharling's emergence, fly through the sky yelping out the news. To hear the hounds of Solarisel on the solstice night is a fortuitous omen for the coming year.

Sign of Solarisel   Sign of Elisin

The deharling is named Elisin, the child of light. He retains this name until the moment of his hostling/lover's death at Cuttingtide.

Rosatide
February 1st

This arojhahn is named for the fact that the trees become rosy with new growth at this time. The last grey white days of winter are marked by the colour of blood as life begins to rise and surge from the earth.

Sign of Eburniel

Elisin is now beginning to grow and his hostling has transformed from his female aspect into Eburniel, the white dehar of the snow covered earth. All early spring flowers, especially those with white petals, are sacred to him. He has nurtured Elisin, borne him from his body and now devotes himself to teaching the deharling the lessons necessary to maturity and eventual solitude. Eburniel teaches Elisin how to imbue the earth with his life-giving energy to encourage new growth.

Traditionally, this is the Arojhahn of Torches, as the rehuna seeks to bring the growing light of the sun into their life. Eburniel is also the light of the candle flame. On Rosatide eve, candles and lamps are lit in every window. The shadowy figure of Eburniel, dressed in a cloak of snow white fur, walks across the fields. His animal is the white wolf, whose breath is freezing mist.

The wistfulness sometimes associated with this arojhahn derives from the fact that, in assuming a more masculine aspect, Eburniel faces the prospect of his own death at Cuttingtide. If the early spring flowers are found sprouting from snow, they are Eburniel's tears. Despite this aspect, Rosatide is a time of hope and promise. As light fills the rehuna's home, so they banish the bleakness of the short days and cold weather.

Bloomtide
March 21st

This arojhahn marks the Spring Equinox. The ascetic Eburniel transforms into the dashing Florinel, who begins to woo the maturing Elisin. He is seen as a lissom young dehar, dressed in green with nut brown hair. Florinel conjures flowers to open with the sound of his voice, which is the music heard in the wind, in spring rains and in the surge of swollen streams as the snow melts. His animal is the white hare. Florinel is a trickster who can sometimes deceive. He leads the unwary into dangerous territory, but can also bestow a change of luck for the better.

Florinel is far too full of life to contemplate such dreary concepts as his own demise. He presides over planting and the reproduction of animals. Elisin is coy and rejects his advances. The only contact Florinel can have with Elisin at this time is to cover his sleeping body with white blossom.

Sign of Florinel

While Florinel's thoughts begin to turn to aruna, Elisin is entranced by the wonder of being alive. His is the unbounded joy of youth, as yet untarnished by adult cares. Bloomtide is the celebration of life for its own sake. On the arojhahn night, the rehuna puts aside fears and uncertainties and focuses on hopes for the future. The light hangs in equal balance, but only for a short time. From this night on, the days lengthen and the air becomes warmer.

Feybraihatide
April 30th/May 1st

This arojhahn is named for the rite of passage harlings undergo as they enter maturity. It is the feast of aruna, of first love and the deep, spiritual passion that enables harlings to be conceived.

Elisin now is full grown, a vision of beauty, like a radiant form of his Shadetide hostling, with fiery red hair. His consort is Feyrahni, but this is properly Elisin's arojhahn, as he is regarded as the presiding dehar. His hostling has now fully transformed into his potential lover. They have barely seen one another since Bloomtide, and now Feyrahni steps from the forest, dark of skin and hair, dressed in clothes made of leather and leaves. His sacred animal is the stag. On Feybraihatide eve, Feyrahni initiates Elisin into the mysteries of aruna and together they create a pearl.

Sign of Feyrahni

Cuttingtide
21st June

This is the Summer Solstice, the moment when the sun begins to decline in strength as it moves away from the earth. Feyrahni becomes the lord of the corn, the sacrificed one, Morterrius. He is at the height of his potency, and therefore in surrendering his life force at this time, the strongest energy enters the earth. Elisin, now with pearl, sheds his youthful name and becomes Shadolan, the hunter, the executioner. Gone are the cares of youth. The sacred animal of the dehara is the hawk.

Morterrius appears as the golden dehar of the corn, with yellow hair. He wears a crown of barley and poppies and is dressed in red and yellow, symbolising the crop and his own blood. Shadolan has a darker aspect, dressed as an archetypal hunter. His beauty is fearsome, his gaze compelling.

On the arojhahn eve, Morterrius walks the fields as a willing sacrifice. In sorrow, Shadolan must take his consort's life. In a grim repetition of Feybraihatide, the lovers meet in a wild place and take aruna together. But its conclusion this time is death. Shadolan's fingernails have become blades that make a thousand cuts in Morterrius' flesh. The dehar stumbles from their trysting place and as he staggers through the fields, so his blood flows down to fertilise the earth. He eventually falls to the ground, which swallows him up, dragging the dehar's body down into itself, so he begins his long journey to the Eternal Plains, the World Beyond, from where he will eventually be reborn as his own son.

Sign of Morterrius   Sign of Shadolan

Reaptide
August 1st

Like Shadetide, this is a time when unusual events are likely to occur. Apparitions can be seen in the fields at mid-day. The landscape holds its breath and the hills become haunted. Shadolan becomes the Field Walker, Verdiferel, wandering in solitude through the ripening crops. His hair is dark and he wears a long robe of earthen colours, decorated with leaves, flowers and heads of wheat. His sacred creature is the white owl, which sweeps through the spectral night and even appears during the day at this time.

Verdiferel, like some of the other seasonal dehara, has a trickster aspect.

One story concerns a har who came upon Verdiferel in a cornfield, apparently making a crop circle. As the har concealed himself and observed, he noticed that the dehar appeared strange, and somewhat unhinged. Verdiferel made decorative talismans from the crop, which he hid around the landscape, in trees and beneath rocks. The observing har knew that these talismans were hidden for hara to find, and that an audience with Verdiferel could be sought this way. He considered himself fortunate to have witnessed where

Verdiferel had concealed the talismans. He took a talisman to a sacred site, which comprised two upright stones supporting a vast slab. Verdiferel was already present in this place, and said he knew the har had come to enquire about his future. He told the har to lie down on the slab. Verdiferel then produced a sickle blade and sliced the har open. He read the future from the entrails. With somewhat dark humour, he said, 'I see you're about to go on a long journey into the otherworld'. He then collected the blood and made a libation in the crop fields. This story suggests that the rehuna should employ caution when asking boons of Verdiferel.

Sign of Verdiferel

Another story concerning this dehar relates that Verdiferel might appear to the rehuna as emerging from the trunk of a tree. He has very long brown hair that comes out of the bark as peculiar strands, and while not as dangerous as other forms of Verdiferel, is extremely haughty. He carries a green orb of light, which is called ozaril. It is said that if the invocation 'Astale ozaril' is chanted, then the light of the dehar goes into the rehuna, enabling them to see the ghosts that walk at noon.

Smoketide
September 21st

This is the autumn equinox and the major harvest arojhahn. The dehar transforms into Prosperiel. He is already a hostling, and in that way fecund. At this time, he appears dressed in garments adorned with autumnal leaves and fruits, and he smells of smoke. He also wears a cloak of fox fur. His sacred animal now is the red fox.

Sign of Prosperiel

Prosperiel, of all the dehara of this half of the year, is the least tricky. Gone are the shadowy aspects of Cuttingtide and Reaptide. He is the expression of fruitfulness, and this is the time of year for the rehuna to make plans for the future, to plant their own seeds of intention that will come to fruit in the New Year.

Shadetide
October 31st

This is the last of the harvest arojhahns, and traditionally a time when the portals between different levels of reality become unstable. It is the time when the veil is thin and discarnate entities can make contact with the living.

At this stage, the dehar transforms into Lachrymide (La-CRIM-ee-day) the Keener. Heavy with pearl and alone, Lachrymide stalks the bare earth. In nature, he can be unpredictable. His tears bring floods and the coldness of his heart brings snow. Only at his arojhahn time does he really show any lighter side, and that is when, compassionate with his own sense of loss, he leads lost souls to the light. It is a night of trickery and feasting, of carnival and costume. Lachrymide is the most intimidating and fearsome of the seasonal dehara, but he is appeased by merriment and feasting.

Lachrymide can be petitioned to give glimpses of the future or news of lost loved ones. After being invoked, he appears at the threshold as a tall har dressed in black with long red hair. Often, his face is veiled.

Sign of Lachrymide

As Lachrymide presides over the dark weeks between Shadetide and the solstice, he is asked to provide warmth, food and shelter, to keep animals healthy through the cold months and to preserve the stored grain. His animal is the black cat, cats being invaluable in guarding grain stores from rats and other vermin. Often, during his reign, tall dark figures are spotted in the fields or at crossroads, or beside lonely tracks. If a rehuna comes across Lachrymide in the dark, they should offer him a gift. If he is pleased with it, he will grant them fortune.

Adkaya
December 7th

This majhahn, two weeks before Natalia, is not one of the major arojhahns, but still an important part of the seasonal calendar. Adkaya observes the time when the dehar Lachrymide drops the pearl of the deharling and transforms into Solarisel, the presiding dehar of Natalia. This is a departure from all the other arojhahns, as the dehar would normally be visualised transforming into the avatar of his new reign as part of the prevailing arojhahn. The pearl of the deharling takes two weeks to mature before giving forth, so the rehuna uses this time to perform majhahns associated with planning and preparation.

Certain of the Panphilien's aspects are associated with smiting and Lachrymide, along with the hunter Shadolan, may be petitioned to deal with enemies and injustice. It is best for a rehuna not to ask boons of Verdiferel, because the results might not be quite what they expect.

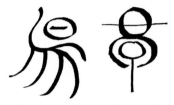

Sign of Lachrymide   Sign of Solarisel

Performing the Seasonal Arojhahns

The texts of the seasonal arojhahns apply to ruhahna, but can be adapted for a rehuna working alone.

While it is preferable for the rehuna to perform the seasonal arojhahns on the exact date, if this is difficult, there is a window of two days on either side. During this time, the energies of the arojhahn are still present, although they at their strongest on the actual day.

In all of the arojhahns, the rehuna creates their Nayati in the usual way, by summoning agmara to flow through them, using the symbols they have learned (incorporating more when they reach further levels) and invoking the four quarter dehara.

Invoking the Dehara Vegrandis of Arotahar

The word 'astale' (a-**star**-lay) is used to invoke the dehara vegrandis. Astale means 'I invoke'. This is combined with the name of the appropriate dehar. E.G. 'Astale Solarisel.' When the rehuna uses this chant, energy is raised in the environment, which is used to 'create' the dehar in the Nayati.

The rehuna should begin the chant as a slow whisper, gradually increasing in volume and pace. As the voice grows louder, and the chant quickens, the rehuna should be aware of energy beginning to whirl around them. This energy is released when the rehuna senses it has reached a peak. At this point, the rehuna throws up their arms with a final cry of the chant, and then places the hands against the ground. They would say, for example: 'Welcome, Solarisel, Come in amity. Come in radiance.'

Raising Energy

For a majhahn of any kind to be effective, it must have a source of power. There are several ways to raise power or energy, and some examples are given here. All require practice to master.

Movement

Some rehunas favour dancing as a method to raise energy. This should be done to hypnotic music, such as tribal drumming. The rehuna should concentrate on the energy moving around them. Once the rehuna decides the power has reached a peak, they release it. This is done by throwing up the arms, with the intention to send the energy to fulfil its purpose, then placing the hands firmly on the ground.

Chanting

The rehuna begins chanting or singing a simple phrase, or rhyme, in a soft whisper. Gradually, as they begin the feel the energy moving around them, they increase the speed, volume and intensity of the chant. Again, when they intuit the moment is right, the energy is released. This method is especially effective for ruhahn.

Percussion

The same effect can be created by using drums, rattles or similar percussive instruments, or simply by clapping the hands. Again, the rehuna should begin softly and slowly, increasing the volume and pace as they raise power. It is most effective when accompanied by chanting and/or movement.

The arojhahns comprise the last part of Neoma. The rehuna will probably be ready to move on to Brynie before they have performed them all, but it is recommended they perform at least two during Neoma, before progressing to the next level. The seasonal arojhahns form the celebratory part of Dehara. While they are not typically used for 'serious' magical work, they may be adapted, if necessary, for the rehuna's particular needs.

Most of the arojhahns include some kind of minor working connected with plans for the future and being in tune with the turning of the seasons, but any of the workings can be substituted or adapted as required.

While some rehunas prefer to continue with the same format for arojhahns, year after year, others prefer variety. Once the rehuna is familiar with the seasonal dehara and their correspondences, they may write their own arojhahns.

Arojhahn Feasts

Traditionally, arojhahns incorporate feasting. A rehuna working alone would probably prefer to partake of the feast within the Nayati, although a ruhahn may elect to feast once the Nayati is dismantled. Both options are appropriate, but at the very least a ruhahn should make a toast within the Nayati after the visualisation or working. The sharing of a cup, which is passed around the Nayati, is a symbol of the union of the ruhahn.

Appropriate foods and drinks for each arojhahn are as follows:

Natalia:

Mulled wine, spiced liqueurs, 'yellow food' to represent sunlight, rich cakes, sumptuous delicacies. This is an arojhahn of indulgence.

Rosatide:

Pale and dairy foods, white cheese, white wine. The arojhahn cup should ideally be milk laced with alcohol, perhaps warmed up.

Bloomtide:

Dairy produce and eggs, including the chocolate variety, and spiced buns. As a toast, a rich and creamy liqueur can be used.

Feybraihatide:

Lush, sensual food and wine are the seasonal components of this feast. Luxury foods, champagne.

Cuttingtide:

Early harvest foods, fresh baked bread, strawberries and cream. Homemade wines, such as elderflower.

Reaptide:

Again, seasonal fruits and fresh bread. Baked potatoes, cheese. Fruity or flowery wines.

Smoketide:

Any foodstuffs made with apples, apple cider or liqueur, rich cakes made with fruit of different kinds, warm bread and yellow butter. Other seasonal fruits, such as pears, plums and berries.

Shadetide:

The late harvest foodstuffs; pies made with pumpkin, or other squashes. Baked root vegetables. Hot soup. Crusty bread. Red wines.

Natalia Arojhahn

Equipment Required (for each present):

Spiced mulled wine
Golden glitter
Gold foil wrapped chocolate money
A candle or tea light (gold or white)

The Nayati should be created in the usual way.

Invoking the Dehar of the Arojhahn

The rehuna stands in the centre of the Nayati, facing inwards. They should raise their arms, close their eyes, draw the sign of Solarisel and visualise the dehar before them. They say:

'Solarisel, dehar of awakening light and renaissance
Whose gaze is the warmth of the new sun
that quickens the earth,
Solarisel, I call you here on this the eve of the New Year,
To continue your reign in this realm.
Reveal to us the deharling of light.
I call you here to reveal to us the mystery of your being
And the cycle of Arotahar.'

All present then chant to evoke Solarisel into the Nayati:
'Astale Solarisel!'

When the invocation is accomplished, all lights in the Nayati are extinguished, except for the light of a fire, if there is one.

The Visualisation

The rehuna prepares as usual for meditation. In ruhahn, one person leads all present in the following meditation. A rehuna working alone may either memorise or tape the meditation beforehand.

Imagine that the backdrop of your surroundings fades away and a new landscape is revealed to you.

The land is held in the grip of an archetypal winter night on Natalia eve. Snow covers the trees and the fields, lying thickly. Even though it is very cold, it is a beautiful scene. Everything sleeps, but you see around you the warm lights from distant dwellings that huddle beneath the hills and at the edges of the forests. In the still air, you catch the faint sounds of merriment; laughter and music.

The fields are bare: all the animals are confined in their barns. Not even an owl crosses the velvet sky, which is filled with stars.

You walk through the snow, hearing the satisfying squeaking crunch beneath your boots. There are no other footsteps to follow. But then, as you walk, you see prints appear in the snow before you, as if an invisible presence is walking ahead of you. They are the prints of long and beautiful feet, and where they fall, so the snow melts a little. It seems the footprints are shining; it's as if sunlight from the summer is captured within them. You catch a faint fragrance of flowers, a reminder of good times past and those yet to come.

You follow the footprints into the dark forest, and presently you come to a glade, where there is an ancient shrine, covered in moss and draped with snow. There is a statue of Panphilien, the dehar who is the embodiment of all the seasonal dehara. He too is robed in snow. In summertime, water flows from his hands, but now it is frozen: an amazing ice sculpture that falls to a stone pool. The light from the stars and the moon falls into the glade. It is very peaceful.

You become aware of a sense of presence. It comes into your heart as a feeling of hope and relief. The cold light of the sky gradually changes to one of golden radiance. Before you, Solarisel materialises. He holds in his arms the perfect deharling Elisin, who is not like a human baby, but appears to be a child of around two years old or so. His eyes, however, contain the wisdom of the ages. Slim white hounds accompany the dehara. They are beautiful, almost like deer.

Elisin beckons to you. He gives you a gift, a symbol of light and hope. The gift is personal to you.

Without speaking aloud, Elisin reveals that every living being is subject to the turning of Arotahar. Light follows darkness, and darkness follows light. It is an eternal cycle, and nothing remains the same, although the cycle itself is perpetual, and in this there is certainty. The only certain thing is change, uncertainty itself. A paradox and a revelation. He says that when the darkness is upon you, it is not for ever, and you should not succumb to dark despair. For without the concept of light, the concept of darkness cannot exist. Even in the darkest times, you are aware of light, simply by its absence, which means it exists for you as potential, always.

Spend some time communing privately with Solarisel and Elisin.

Now, Solarisel leads the way from the forest. In the east, you see the first flush of dawn in the sky. At the sight of it, Solarisel's hounds begin to bay and cry. Their song wakes up the land. The sun rises, bright and clear, and you are bathed in its radiance. It is like a cleansing bath of light, filling you up with optimism, raising your spirits. Really feel that anything is possible, that the new sun brings the promise of beneficial change. Think about your plans for the year ahead, imbue them with the providence of the sun, of the dehara of Natalia, which means birth.

Go now to one of the settlements in the area. Even though you have not slept, you are not tired. Join a harish community in celebration of the season. Already you can smell the tempting aroma of spiced breakfast cakes on the air. Spend some time in free visualisation, doing as you wish. When you are ready to return to normal consciousness, open your eyes.

The Working

The rehuna lights a small candle, saying something appropriate as to what that action means to them. (I.e.: *'I kindle this light to bring abundance to my life. In the names of Solarisel and Elisin, it will be so.'*) The rehuna should cup their hands around the light for a few moments, seeing how the candle flame illumines their skin. They should focus on taking that light into themselves.

For ruhahn: An officiating rehuna passes round a plate of chocolate money wrapped in gold. To each person, they say, *'You will never hunger'*, before a coin is taken.

For an individual: Before taking a coin, the rehuna should say, *'I will never hunger.'*

As the rehuna unwraps the coin, they should visualise that they are unwrapping a gift from the dehara themselves, a magical food that brings luck and abundance. As the rehuna eats it, they should visualise taking that power into themselves. Chocolate is a food of the gods, sumptuous and silky. It represents all good things in life.

For a group: The officiating rehuna then sprinkles each head with a few grains of golden glitter, saying, 'You will forever shine with abundance and richness, in all its forms.'

For an individual: The rehuna sprinkles themselves with glitter, saying: 'I will forever shine with abundance and richness, in all its forms.'

The rehuna should close their eyes and imagine this glittering colour as a powerful dust of the dehara. It bestows all the riches of life.

Finally, the rehuna should drink of the mulled wine. A ruhahn may pass it around between them, making a toast, as appropriate. The feast may be partaken of now, or after the Nayati is dismantled.

Dismantling the Nayati

The rehuna stands in the centre of the room, raises arms and says,

> *'Solarisel and Elisin, shining dehara of the season,*
> *Symbols of hope and abundance,*
> *Guardians of Arotahar.*
> *Your knowledge is respected and revered*
> *I now release you from this Nayati*
> *To continue your reign.*
> *Walk as you will, in this world and all others.'*

Now the Nayati is fully dismantled in the usual manner.

Rosatide Arojhahn

Preparation:

The rehuna should place a small candle or a lantern in every window of their dwelling where it's possible, but should leave them unlit. Later, they will be lit and left to burn away, so it should be ensured that any candles are in a safe place and can't set fire to anything or get knocked over.

The rehuna creates the Nayati in the usual manner.

When this is done, the rehuna stands in the centre of the Nayati, draws the sign of Solarisel and visualises the gold and white form of the dehar appearing before them. The rehuna says to him:

> *'Solarisel, your time in this realm has come to an end.*
> *The power you wielded must pass on to Eburniel,*
> *Who shall be called here to continue the cycle of Arotahar.*
> *Solarisel, though your ascendancy has ended,*
> *You are not forgotten, and will we meet again*
> *at the appointed time,*
> *When once more you shall reign over the season.'*

The rehuna should be silent for a minute. Solarisel bows to them and gradually fades away.

Invoking the Dehara of the Arojhahn

The rehuna stands in the centre of the Nayati, facing inwards. They should raise arms, close eyes, draw the sign of Eburniel and visualise the dehar. He is seen as a tall sombre figure dressed in a long hooded coat or cloak of white wolf fur. The hood nearly covers his face, but the lower half can be seen. The rehuna concentrates on this image and says:

> *'Eburniel, dehar of the of the snow covered earth*
> *White Walker of the Fields,*
> *I call you here this night*
> *To witness the Arojhahn of Torches.*
> *I call you here to reveal to me the mystery of your being*
> *And the cycle of the seasons.'*

The rehuna visualises Eburniel manifesting before them, accompanied by his sacred animal, the white wolf.

Eburniel is evoked into the Nayati by the following chant:

> *'Astale Eburniel!'*

The Visualisation

The rehuna prepares as usual for meditation. In ruhahn, one person leads all present in the following meditation. A rehuna working alone may either memorise or tape the meditation beforehand.

Imagine the backdrop of your surroundings fading away and a new landscape being revealed to you.

See a northern landscape covered in snow. It is dusk and the land glows strangely in the dim light. Feel the chill air against your skin and in your lungs. If you performed the majhahn at Natalia, this is the place you came to out of the wilderness to witness the rebirth of the sun. But now that dawn seems far away, for the land is hard and dead, the first growth has yet to struggle out of the darkness.

Walk through this landscape. A ground mist tumbles over

and around your feet, and the air becomes foggy, but in the distance you can perceive the faint lights of various farmsteads and dwellings.

You hear the howl of a wolf and then, as you squint your eyes, you see shapes emerging from the mist. It is Eburniel, accompanied by his sacred beast, the wolf, and also by a smaller figure, who is the harling Elisin. It is Eburniel's task to teach his son all that he'll need to know for his role in Arotahar. Eburniel shows Elisin the spots of power in the lanscape, the places where soon new life will grow.

You follow them and watch as Elisin places his hands against the cold earth, filling it with the life force, which encourages all things to thrive. Eburniel stands over him protectively and proudly, yet you can feel his sadness as if it were your own. The prime of life has yet to come, but even so, these early days of the year carry within them the seeds of death. In teaching Elisin, Eburniel is nurturing his own executioner. But he knows that is the way it must be: that for eternity they will represent and enact the cycle of birth, death and rebirth.

Walk with the dehara now, and see if there are any messages or gifts for you at this time. Give yourself several minutes for this.

Visualise now that the dawn is approaching, and from all the dwellings around you, hara come forth bearing torches, lighting up the land. They are chanting softly, a wistful song that also has within it the promise of joy and hope. It is so beautiful that it affects you deeply. For just a moment, you become aware of the immensity of creation, the endless cycles of time, your own place within the whole.

As you gaze at the dark silhouettes of the trees around you, it seems as if they pulse with a faint ruby glow. It is the lifeblood of the land, the sap beginning to rise.

The sun rises red on the horizon and you watch as Eburniel walks away from his son, who barely seems to notice, as he is so interested in all that he feels and hears around him. Only you see the last backward glance that

Eburniel gives the harling. Where his tears fall, so the most delicate white flowers push out of the snow.

As the sun rises higher, the melancholy aspect of the season melts away. Hara celebrate the return of life and call to Elisin to wake the land from its slumber. Spend a few moments now thinking about what the coming year will bring for you and how you can shape its potential. Drink of the energy of the season, the stirring of life and energy, which will soon burst forth from potential into reality. Now is the time to sow your dreams.

Join one of the groups of hara and return with them to their home. You can spend some time with them to experience their celebration and learn more of their cycle of the seasons.

When you are ready, return to normal consciousness, ground yourself and open your eyes.

The Working

Before leaving the Nayati, the rehuna should imagine that there is a magical portal they can walk through. This does not disrupt the energy fabric of the Nayati.

The rehuna should proceed from room to room lighting the candles left previously in the windows. In each room, they should say, 'May the light of returning life fill my domain and my being.'

The rehuna should spend a few moments, with closed eyes, in each room to visualise their dwelling filling with light, which is a beacon to positive forces. This light banishes all shadows of doubt and fear.

The candles should be left to burn away. The rehuna should not snuff them out unless they really have to, and then it should be done with the fingers, saying, 'As the flame dies, so the light lives on.'

Then the rehuna should return to the Nayati and seal the portal they made in whatever way feels appropriate.

The rehuna makes a toast to the dehara. The feast may be

partaken of now, or after the Nayati is dismantled.

Dismantling the Nayati

The rehuna stands in the centre of the room, raises arms and says,

> *'Eburniel and Elisin, shining dehara of the season,*
> *Symbols of hope and potential,*
> *Guardians of Arotahar.*
> *Your knowledge is respected and revered*
> *I now release you from this Nayati*
> *To continue your reign.*
> *Walk as you will, in this world and all others.'*

Now the Nayati is fully dismantled in the usual manner.

Bloomtide Arojhahn

Equipment Required

A small chocolate egg
A sharp implement with which to inscribe a sigil
on the egg

The rehuna creates the Nayati in the usual manner.

When this is done, the rehuna stands in the centre of the Nayati, draws the sign of Eburniel and visualises the dehar appearing before them. The rehuna says to him:

> 'Eburniel, your time in this realm has come to an end.
> The power you wielded must pass on to Florinel,
> Who shall be called here to continue the cycle of Arotahar.
> Eburniel, though your ascendancy has ended,
> You are not forgotten, and will we meet again
> at the appointed time,
> When once more you shall reign over the season.'

The rehuna should be silent for a minute. Eburniel bows to them and gradually fades away.

Invoking the Dehara of the Arojhahn

For this arojhahn, the rehuna invokes both dehara, as Elisin is now formed enough to have a separate presence.

The rehuna stands in the centre of the Nayati, facing inwards. They should raise their arms, and draw the sign of Elisin upon the air. Then they should close their eyes, and first visualise the dehar appearing. He is seen as a harling, older than he was at Rosatide. It can be seen in his face the dehar he will become. The rehuna may imagine him dressed as they will, but should focus on the vibrant energy that emanates from him. He is promise for the future. As he is invoked, the rehuna should be aware of Elisin's attributes strongly, that anything is possible with the hope and joy of youth on their side. Elisin has yet to encounter any of life's trials. He is pure and innocent. The rehuna concentrates on this image and says, aloud or in the mind:

'Elisin, Child of Light
Heart of the Lengthening Days,
I call you here this night to witness this rite.
I call you here to reveal to me the mystery of your being
And the cycle of the seasons.'

Elisin is invoked into the Nayati by chanting the following:

'Astale Elisin!'

Now the rehuna calls upon Florinel, as for Elisin, also using the appropriate sign before invocation. Florinel is seen as a lissom young har, dressed in green with nut brown hair. Florinel conjures flowers to open with the sound of his voice, which is the music heard in the wind, in spring rains and in the chatter of swollen streams as the snow melts. His animal is the white hare.

'Florinel, Lord of the Forest Ways,
Who is the beauty of nature,
I call you here this night to witness this rite.
I call you here to reveal to me the mystery of your being
And the cycle of the seasons.'

The chant for him is: *'Astale Florinel.'*

The Visualisation

Prepare as you normally to do meditate. Imagine the backdrop of your surroundings fading away and a new landscape being revealed to you.

You find yourself in the place you saw the last time you visited this realm at Rosatide, but now the snow has gone. All around you, the land is waking up after its winter sleep. Breathe deep, take in the essence of the season with its myriad scents of freshness and earth.

See Elisin ahead of you. At once you are affected by his boundless enthusiasm for life, his lack of care or worry. Feel your spirits lift. It's as if Elisin's joy rubs off on you. The anxieties of your life cannot exist in this realm. Here, you are free of them. Experience this as fully as you can. Where Elisin walks, the land blooms.

As you follow the dehar, you become aware that he is being watched by Florinel from the shadows of a forest. You can feel the yearning emanating from Florinel, who has transformed from the dour Eburniel into a younger har, not that much older than Elisin. Elisin is totally unaware of his admirer. The potential of their union is still just a dream in the heart of the earth.

Spend some time in the world of your visualisation, soaking up the atmosphere of the season and its associations.

When you are ready, return to normal consciousness and open your eyes.

The Working

The rehuna creates a sigil embodying their wishes for the future. They should carve this sigil into the chocolate egg, visualising as they do so that their entire intention pours into it, making the egg a magical tool. The rehuna should send to the dehara their hopes and desires. They should imagine sealing them within a pearl that with the warmth of will and intention will soon hatch.

The rehuna should raise energy through chanting or dancing and direct this into the egg.

Then the rehuna should consume the egg, taking into themselves its power.

The rehuna makes a toast to the dehara. The feast may be partaken of now, or after the Nayati is dismantled.

Dismantling the Nayati

The rehuna stands in the centre of the Nayati, raises arms and says,

> *'Elisin, Child of Light,*
> *Florinel, Lord of the Forest Ways,*
> *Guardians of Arotahar.*
> *Your knowledge is respected and revered*
> *I now release you from this Nayati*
> *To continue your reign.*
> *Walk as you will, in this world and all others.'*

The Nayati is then dismantled in the usual manner.

Feybraihatide Arojhahn

Equipment (for each participant)

A piece of paper and something to write with.

The rehuna creates the Nayati in the usual manner.

When this is done, the rehuna stands in the centre of the Nayati, draws the sign of Florinel upon the air and visualises the dehar appearing before them. The rehuna says to him:

> 'Florinel, your time in this realm has come to an end.
> The power you wielded must pass on to Feyrahni,
> Who shall be called here to continue the cycle of Arotahar.
> Florinel, though your ascendancy has ended,
> You are not forgotten, and will we meet again
> at the appointed time,
> When once more you shall reign over the season.'

The rehuna should be silent for a minute. Florinel bows to them and gradually fades away.

Invoking the Dehara of the Arojhahn

For this arojhahn, both dehara are invoked, as for Bloomtide.

The rehuna stands in the centre of the Nayati, facing inwards. They draw the sign of Elisin upon the air, raise their arms, close eyes, and visualize the dehar before them. He is now a radiant young har of great beauty, brimming with energy, and newly mature. Just to look upon him kindles sexual desire. The rehuna concentrates on this image and says:

96

'Elisin, dehar of beauty
Who inflames the souls of all who look upon you,
I call you here this night to witness this rite.
I call you here to reveal to me the mystery of your being
And the cycle of the seasons.'

Elisin is invoked into the Nayati with the following chant:

'Astale Elisin!'

The rehuna now calls upon Feyrahni, as for Elisin, using the appropriate sign. He is seen as a lithe har, dark of hair and skin, dressed in clothes made of leather and leaves. His sacred animal is the stag.

'Feyrahni, soft of foot and dark of eye,
who presides over the secret glades,
I call you here this night to witness this rite.
I call you here to reveal to me the mystery of your being
And the cycle of the seasons.'

The chant for the dehar is: *'Astale Feyrahni.'*

The Visualisation

Prepare as you normally to do meditate. Imagine the backdrop of your surroundings fading away and a new landscape being revealed to you.

You find yourself in the place you saw the last time you visited this realm at Bloomtide, but now the season has moved on, and the trees are heavy with blossom. The air smells fresh and is warmer now. Breathe deep, take in the essence of the season with its myriad scents of freshness and earth.

See Elisin walking through the fields at dusk, among the animals whose young are being born. Imagine that his power surrounds him as a nimbus of soft light and his skin exudes a heavy perfume. His hair is wound with blossom, trailing down his back, and his feet are bare. As you gaze upon him, become aware of your own power, your own sexuality, that blooms at this time of year. You have the power to create; not just new life, but in all manner of other ways too. What begin as ideas become actual. Inspiration becomes a work of art, an artefact, a finished project.

Think about what you wish to create through the year and visualise that the creative energy of the season permeates your thoughts, your being, your life.

Elisin walks into the dark forest, and you follow him. On this night, hara are celebrating their own rites, and you catch glimpses of lights through the trees: lanterns and torches. Perhaps you hear laughter, and the sound of running feet.

You see Feyrahni appear from the shadows, tall and lean, dressed as a hunter. Elisin becomes aware of Feyrahni's intense stare and bounds away from him, luring Feyrahni to pursue him.

Follow them, and witness the chase, the inevitable yielding. At this time, Elisin experiences aruna for the first time, and conceives a pearl with Feyrahni, that will grow into the young god of the winter solstice. Later in the year, at midsummer, Elisin will take the life of his consort in order to fertilise the fields, but for this night, he and Feyrahni are free of such cares.

Spend some time in the world of your visualisation, soaking up the atmosphere of the season and its associations. If you wish to, join in with a group of hara to celebrate Feybraihatide in your own way.

When you are ready, return to normal consciousness and open your eyes.

The Working

The conception of a project includes a variety of creative ideas. The rehuna should think about the project they most wish to conceive and realise. This might be for themselves or for others. The separate components should be written as words or drawn as sigils or pictures on the paper previously put aside for this purpose. The marks should form an interlinking pattern, symbolising that the project will be bigger than the sum of its parts. It is symbolic of the union of

Feyrahni and Elisin. The rehuna holds the paper between their hands and in their own words, calls upon the dehara to fill it with the power of creativity. They should visualise this power going into the words they have written.

The paper or papers should then be folded and placed in the centre of the Nayati. Energy should be raised and directed into them, and then the papers should be burned. As the flames consume them, so the desires or the rehuna are sent into the ethers.

The rehuna makes a toast to the dehara. The feast may be partaken of now, or after the Nayati is dismantled.

Dismantling the Nayati

The rehuna stands in the centre of the Nayati, raises arms and says,

> 'Elisin, Beauty of Life,
> Feyrahni, Lord of the Secret Glades,
> Guardians of Arotahar.
> Your knowledge is respected and revered
> I now release you from this Nayati
> To continue your reign.
> Walk as you will, in this world and all others.'

The Nayati is then dismantled in the usual manner.

Cuttingtide Arojhahn

Equipment (for each participant):

A piece of paper and something to write with.

The rehuna creates the Nayati in the usual manner.

When this is done, the rehuna stands in the centre of the Nayati, draws the signs of Feyrahni and Elisin, and visualises the dehara appearing before them. The rehuna says to them:

'Feyrahni, Elisin: your time in this realm has come to an end.
The power you wielded must pass on
to Morterrius and Shadolan,
Who shall be called here to continue the cycle of Arotahar.
Dehara, though your ascendancy has ended,
You are not forgotten, and will we meet again
at the appointed time,
When once more you shall reign over the season.'

The rehuna should be silent for a minute. Feyrahni and Elisin bow to them and gradually fade away.

Invoking the Dehara of the Arojhahn

The rehuna stands in the centre of the Nayati, facing inwards. They draw the sign of Shadolan upon the air, raise their arms, close eyes, and visualise the dehar before them. He is seen as beautiful but quite fearsome, an archetypal hunter, dressed in close-fitting garments of animal hide. He is accompanied by a hawk. The rehuna concentrates on this image and says:

> *'Shadolan, He Who Walks the Furrows in Darkness.*
> *Shadolan, fatal lover*
> *I call to you this night, come forth*
> *And witness this rite.*
> *Reveal to us the mystery of your being and of the seasons.'*

Shadolan is invoked into the Nayati with the following chant:

> *'Astale, Shadolan!'*

Now the rehuna calls upon Morterrius, using the appropriate sign. He is seen as golden haired with a crown of barley and red poppies. His garments are yellow and red.

> *'Morterrius, Life of the Land*
> *Beauty of Nature,*
> *You who give your blood in sacrifice*
> *I call to you this night, come forth*
> *And witness this rite.*
> *Reveal to us the mystery of your being and of the seasons.'*

The chant for the dehar is: *'Astale Morterrius!'*

The Working

As previous arojhahns have involved the projection of desires and hopes, at Cuttingtide the emphasis shifts. The rehuna should take the piece of paper previously set aside and contrive a sigil or series of linked pictures and words to depict the things they perceive as weaknesses and obstacles within themselves, aspects that hold them back in life. As they create this magical tool, they should say, repeatedly: 'I name you (weakness/fear/insecurity, etc.)', listing all they things they wish to cut from their lives. When this is complete, the paper or papers are set folded upon the altar.

The Visualisation

Prepare as usual for a meditation, with breathing and relaxation.

See a new landscape forming before your inner eye, the landscape of high summer. This is the longest day of the year, and the eve when Shadolan takes the life of his lover/hostling, who is now Morterrius.

You are walking through a wheat field, and the sun is beginning to set across the land. There are dark groves of tall oak trees to either side of the field, where the shadows have already gathered. You watch them nervously, from the corner of your eye.

You perceive a movement in the darkness and as you turn to look, you see a figure emerging from the trees, a tall har robed in a green so dark it looks black. His deep red hair is the colour of dried blood and is wound with heads of wheat. He emanates an air of wistfulness, yet you can tell he is not in despair. He is the willing sacrifice to the land, and even in these last moments, he knows he will be reborn in the future. His sureness can give you hope about your own life. What might seem terrible and eternal in the moment is only a passing phase. Summer always follows winter, and without the dark and cold, we cannot appreciate the delights of light and heat.

Now you walk behind Morterrius through the rows of wheat, which is so tall it comes above your waist. From this night on, the dark will draw in, leading you to the cold months of winter, when all is dead and barren. It seems inconceivable on this warm balmy evening, when the trees are in full leaf and the air full of the scents of summer. But this is the night of summer's death and ahead of you, Morterrius leaves a chill trail in the air, as he is the portent of this time.

You hear a high pitched scream, which alarms you, but when you look up you see it is only a wide-winged hawk. It hangs in the air above Morterrius, who has now stopped walking. This is his sacred animal, but also that of his consort, Shadolan. The hawk's appearance indicates that Shadolan approaches.

You see a tall slim figure dressed in green and gold emerge from the woods on the other side of the field. This is the hunter, who was born at the winter solstice as Elisin and has now reached full maturity. As the winter solstice heralds birth, so its opposite heralds death.

Shadolan approaches Morterrius and they embrace, each aware of the significance of this night. The consummate their last act of love in this season, but it concludes with Shadolan taking Morterrius' life. His fingernails have become blades that make a thousand cuts upon Morterrius' body. It does not kill him instantly, but once it is done, and Morterrius' blood has begun to soak into the field, Shadolan runs back like a ghost into the trees. He is already with pearl, and will host the birth of the new sun at the winter solstice.

You stand over the body of Morterrius, perhaps tempted to help stem the blood that pours from his wounds, but you see a faint smile upon his pale face and know you cannot interfere in this cycle. The least you can do is offer support as Morterrius opens his eyes and tries to get to his feet. You know he must walk the fields until his blood has flowed entirely into the land. Only then may he find rest.

As you walk with Morterrius, he might talk with you, give you advice for the coming winter, which as yet seems far away. Give yourself some time for this.

Eventually, Morterrius succumbs to his injuries and sinks down upon the ground. As you watch the earth opens up, and almost in a caressing manner, enfolds Morterrius' body and takes him back into itself. There is nothing to mark his grave and soon the ground looks as if it had never been disturbed.

As you stand over this unmarked spot, you think about how sometimes it is necessary to relinquish before you can gain. Morterrius' sacrifice is a symbol. If you can let go of all that holds you back, grinds you down and burdens you, you will find the strength and freedom to walk into any situation.

See the landscape fade away and return to your own reality as normal.

Once the rehuna has opened their eyes, they should take up the piece of folded paper they wrote upon and burn it. As they watch it burn, they should visualise and intend that the negative qualities are being taken away into the ethers.

The rehuna makes a toast to the dehara. The feast may be partaken of now, or after the Nayati is dismantled.

Dismantling the Nayati

The rehuna stands in the centre of the Nayati, raises their arms and says:

> *'Shadolan, Walker of the Furrows,*
> *Guardian of Arotahar.*
> *Your knowledge is respected and revered*
> *I now release you from this Nayati*
> *To continue your reign.*
> *Walk as you will, in this world and all others.'*

The Nayati is then dismantled in the usual manner.

Reaptide Arojhahn

There is no specific working for this arojhahn, but a rehuna or ruhahn can devise one to be inserted after the visualisation if there is work they wish to perform at this time.

The rehuna creates the Nayati in the usual manner.

When this is done, the rehuna stands in the centre of the Nayati, draws the sign of Shadolan upon the air and visualises the dehar appearing before them. The rehuna says to him:

'Shadolan, your time in this realm has come to an end.
The power you wielded must pass on to Verdiferel,
Who shall be called here to continue the cycle of Arotahar.
Shadolan, though your ascendancy has ended,
You are not forgotten, and will we meet again
at the appointed time,
When once more you shall reign over the season.'

The rehuna should be silent for a minute. Shadolan bows to them and gradually fades away.

Invoking the Dehar of the Arojhahn

Because of the nature of Verdiferel, the rehuna should first construct the Nayati to contain him. The rehuna stands in the centre of their working space and prepares for meditation in the usual way.

Visualise yourself in a landscape of hills around a valley. In the centre of the valley is a wide pool. It is sundown on the eve of Reaptide. Around you, hara are lighting beacon fires on the hills. Above you the moon hangs full. You are the hienama of this ceremony, but you might perhaps want your own hienama with you for this rite.

The hara begin to chant in low voices, which gradually rise in volume. Add your voice to theirs. You are calling the Reaptide moon down into the pool, which is also Verdiferel. As you do this, the Nightmanes appear, spectral black horses galloping silently around the pool, conjuring their own vortex of energy.

When you feel the container is empowered, raise your arms and visualise Verdiferel. He is the dehar of deep summer, clad in green and the yellow of ripening corn. His hair trails behind him, full of grasses and leaves. Concentrate on this image and draw the sign of Verdiferel in the air or upon the mind's eye. Say, aloud or in your mind:

> *'Verdiferel, Spirit of the of the Noontide of Ghosts*
> *Field Walker, Phantom of the Corn,*
> *I call you here this night*
> *To witness the Arojhahn of Reaptide.*
> *I call you here to reveal to us the mystery of your being*
> *And the cycle of the seasons.'*

Visualise Verdiferel manifesting before you, accompanied by his totem animal, the white owl. Raise power to help summon and empower this entity, by chanting, circling, dancing or whatever method you generally use.

Evoke Verdiferel into your Nayati by chanting the following:

> *'Astale, Verdiferel!'*

When the power has been released, the rehuna should say to Verdiferel: 'Verdiferel, dehar of the Reaptide, you are welcome here in your compassionate form, but know you are subject to our will. You may not cause harm in this Nayati, nor among its rehunas. This is law, in the name of the

Aghama, the fifth element, the star and your master.'

The Visualisation

The rehuna now returns to the meditation.

It is the day following the containment majhahn, under whose spell Verdiferel is still confined. This is the landscape of the depths of summer, when the trees are in full leaf and the crops ripen. The air is full of insects and the scents of the season. Downy seeds float on the air and everything is fecund, burgeoning, heavy with juice and sap. Even as you emerge into this world, you sense immense shimmering power around you. The trees seem unnaturally tall and broad. Your surroundings shiver with sentience, and you catch glimpses of swift smoky shapes, as if unseen things move at the edge of your perception.

In this season, Verdiferel walks the land, and any who come close to him is filled with irrational dread as well as awe. His power and the power of nature are one. Verdiferel is in some ways the most potent of the seasonal dehara. For a short time, he is unencumbered by cares, free to enjoy his own power, to revel in it. This is the time when ghosts walk the hills at mid-day, and you should be wary of the stranger you meet upon your path. Verdiferel can be a trickster who can lead the incautious onto dangerous paths. But those who are brave enough to follow him can be shown great wonders.

Go now to seek Verdiferel. Walk through forests, fields and hills, past sleeping settlements and farms. Seek him out in the sweltering heat and discover what he will reveal to you. Look for the place where the white owl flies by day.

Spend time exploring the landscape, and see if there are any messages for you at this time. When you meet Verdiferel, deal with him commandingly. Treat his words as riddles and be careful of taking any gift he offers you. Remember your own hienama can protect you, so if Verdiferel misbehaves, let your hienama take control.

When you are ready, return to normal consciousness, ground yourself and open your eyes.

The rehuna makes a toast to the dehara. The feast may be partaken of now, or after the Nayati is dismantled.

Dismantling the Nayati

The rehuna stands in the centre of the Nayati, raises arms and says,

> *'Verdiferel, Spirit of the Noontide of Ghosts*
> *Field Walker, Phantom of the Corn,*
> *Guardian of Arotahar.*
> *Your knowledge is respected and revered*
> *I now release you from this Nayati*
> *To continue your reign.*
> *Walk as you will, in this world and all others.'*

The Nayati is now dismantled in the usual manner.

Smoketide Arojhahn

From the Summer Solstice onwards, the light has been retreating from the land. At the Autumn Equinox, as with the Spring Equinox, the light hangs in equal balance. These arojhahns are nexus points, moments of stillness in the wheel of the year.

The flowers of the earth are fading now, and the trees are beginning to change. Life retreats into darkness, but this is also the time of the major harvest arojhahn. The land has given up its bounty, which is stored for the long winter months.

As with the previous majhahn, there is no set working for Smoketide, although a rehuna or ruhahn can insert one if they wish after the visualisation. This is the time of preparation for the harsh winter and both Reaptide and Smoketide are celebrations of harvest. At such times, it is beneficial for a rehuna to meditate upon the things they have achieved in their own lives.

The rehuna creates the Nayati in the usual manner.

When this is done, the rehuna stands in the centre of the Nayati, draws the sign of Verdiferel and visualises the dehar appearing before them. The rehuna says to him:

> *'Verdiferel, your time in this realm has come to an end.*
> *The power you wielded must pass on to Prosperiel,*
> *Who shall be called here to continue the cycle of Arotahar.*
> *Verdiferel, though your ascendancy has ended,*

You are not forgotten, and will we meet again
at the appointed time,
When once more you shall reign over the season.'

The rehuna should be silent for a minute. Verdiferel bows to them and gradually fades away.

Invoking the Dehar of the Arojhahn

The rehuna stands in the centre of the Nayati, facing inwards. They should draw the sign of Prosperiel upon the air, raise their arms, close eyes, and visualize the dehar appearing before them. He is seen as standing tall, in clothes covered in, or made of, late flowers, small fruits, and leaves, which are covered by a long cloak or coat of fox fur. He is accompanied by his totem animal, the red fox. A pearl grows within him, and as such he represents the ideas planted at this time for later growth. Concentrate on this image and say, aloud or in your mind:

'*Prosperiel, Dehar of Plenty*
Dehar of Promise
Heart of the Shortening Days,
I call you here this night to witness this rite.
I call you here to reveal to us the mystery of your being
And the cycle of the seasons.'

The rehuna evokes Prosperiel into the Nayati by chanting the following:

'*Astale, Prosperiel!'*

The Visualisation

Prepare as you normally to do meditate. Imagine the backdrop of your surroundings fading away and a new landscape being revealed to you.

You find yourself in the place you saw the last time you visited this realm at Reaptide, but now the intense heavy greenery of summer is fading. All around you, the land is preparing for its winter slumber, although before it does so, it will go out in a blaze of glory – its autumn finery. Breathe deep, take in the essence of the season with its myriad scents of ripeness and earth. Smell the scent of approaching fall in the air, the aroma of smoke.

Find yourself walking through the fields and forests with Prosperiel at your side. Feel emanating from him the energy of life, for he represents part of the eternal wheel of birth, life, death and rebirth. Talk with him and listen to what he has to say to you.

For this arojhahn, it's appropriate to visualise taking part in some kind of harvest celebration with hara of the inner world.

The emotion of this arojhahn is a kind of staunch yet joyful resignation, being prepared for anything that winter might throw at you, sure that you have made the proper provisions. Before winter sets in, you can enjoy the weeks of colour and perfume, the riotous display of the fall. You can begin to make preparations for the biggest arojhahns of the year, Shadetide and Natalia.

Spend some time in the world of your visualisation, soaking up the atmosphere of the season and its associations.

When you are ready, return to normal consciousness and open your eyes.

The rehuna makes a toast to the dehara. The feast may be partaken of now, or after the Nayati is dismantled.

Dismantling the Nayati

The rehuna stands in the centre of the Nayati, raises their arms and says:

'Prosperiel, Dehar of Plenty and Abundance,
Guardian of Arotahar.
Your knowledge is respected and revered

115

I now release you from this Nayati
To continue your reign.
Walk as you will, in this world and all others.'

The Nayati is now dismantled in the usual manner.

Shadetide Arojhahn

This is the last of the harvest arojhahns, and traditionally a time when the portals between different levels of reality become unstable. It is the time when the veil is thin and discarnate entities can make contact with the living.

Equipment

Some tools for scrying and divination, such as Tarot cards, a bowl of ink, or some other method of the rehuna's own devising.

The rehuna creates the Nayati in the usual manner.

When this is done, the rehuna stands in the centre of the Nayati, draws the sign of Prosperiel upon the air and visualises the dehar appearing before them. The rehuna says to him:

'Prosperiel, your time in this realm has come to an end.
The power you wielded must pass on to Lachrymide,
Who shall be called here to continue the cycle of Arotahar.
Prosperiel, though your ascendancy has ended,
You are not forgotten, and will we meet again
at the appointed time,
When once more you shall reign over the season.'

118

The rehuna should be silent for a minute. Prosperiel bows to them and gradually fades away.

Invoking the Dehar of the Arojhahn

The rehuna stands in the centre of the Nayati, facing inwards. They draw the sign of Lachrymide upon the air, raise their arms, close eyes, and visualise the dehar appearing before them. He is seen beyond the boundary of the Nayati: a very tall dehar, who is veiled, but whose red hair shows through his thin dark veil.

> *'Lachrymide, Dehar of Darkness and Fire*
> *He Who Sees Beyond the Veil,*
> *I call you here this night to witness this rite.*
> *I call you here to reveal to us the mystery of your being*
> *And the cycle of the seasons.'*

Lachrymide is invoked into the Nayati by the following chant:

> *'Astale Lachrymide!'*

The Visualisation

Prepare as you normally to do meditate. Imagine the backdrop of your surroundings fading away and a new landscape being revealed to you.

The land is now dark and cold, as winter draws in. Lachrymide walks the fields alone, a dark and shadowy figure. Lost souls are drawn to him, and he can direct them to where they should be.

Approach him and ask him to reveal to you glimpses of the future. Remember he can be a trickster, so approach him with confidence and command him.

Spend some time in this realm, walking with the dehar, to see what he shows to you. He is fearsome, but he is also grieving and because of that has compassion.

When you are ready to return to normal consciousness, open your eyes.

119

The Working

The rehuna now composes themselves to scry and uses whatever tools they have previously set aside for this purpose.

The rehuna makes a toast to the dehara. The feast may be partaken of now, or after the Nayati is dismantled.

Dismantling the Nayati

The rehuna stands in the centre of the room, raises their arms and says:

'Lachrymide,
Dehar of Shadows,
Hostling of the Pearl of Hope,
Guardian of Arotahar.
Your knowledge is respected and revered
I now release you from this Nayati
To continue your reign.
Walk as you will, in this world and all others.'

The Nayati is then dismantled in the usual manner.

Adkaya Majhahn

As the pearl containing the deharling Elisin is dropped two weeks before Natalia, it's appropriate that the transference of reign from Lachrymide to Solarisel should be performed at this time. Also, the rehuna visualises the pearl manifesting into being.

The rehuna creates the Nayati in the usual manner.

Once this is done, the rehuna stands in the centre of the Nayati, draws the sign of Lachrymide upon the air and visualises the tall dark form of the dehar appearing before them. The rehuna says:

> *'Lachrymide, your time in this realm has come to an end.*
> *The power you wielded must pass on to Solarisel,*
> *Who shall be called here to continue the cycle of Arotahar.*
> *Lachrymide, though your ascendancy has ended,*
> *You are not forgotten, and will we meet again*
> *at the appointed time,*
> *When once more you shall reign over the season.'*

The rehuna is silent for a minute. Lachrymide then bows to them and gradually fades away.

The rehuna stands in the centre of the Nayati, facing inwards. They should draw the sign of Solarisel upon the air, raise their arms, close their eyes, and visualise the dehar appearing before them. They say:

'Solarisel, Dehar of the Light's Potential,
Hostling and Protector of all Future Hope,
I call you here this night to begin your reign in this realm.
I call you here to reveal to me the mystery of your being
And the cycle of Arotahar.
I call you here that I might witness
the manifestation of the pearl of light.'

The rehuna then chants to evoke Solarisel into the Nayati:

'Astale Solarisel!'

The Visualisation

Prepare as you normally to do meditate. Imagine the backdrop of your surroundings fading away and a new landscape being revealed to you.

You find yourself within a rustic Nayati, deep in the heart of a winter forest. The Nayati is decorated with freshly cut boughs of pine, and their scent fills the air.

An area has been prepared, in which Solarisel may give forth the pearl containing the deharling, Elisin. Solarisel is attended by a group of nine hienamas, who direct agmara into him, and chant to facilitate the process. Other hara have gathered in the Nayati to witness the event in silence. They hold candles or lamps, which provide the only light, and stand well back from the place where Solarisel lies.

You too stand beyond the circle of Solarisel's attendants, in the knowledge that what you are witnessing is sacred and essential. As you gaze upon Solarisel's face, which is creased with pain, different aspects of Panphilien flicker across his features. For brief moments, you catch glimpses of all the different aspects of the dehar, even Elisin himself.

Eventually, the pearl is expelled and one of the attendants holds it up for all to see. It glows with a soft light, like the first rays of the sun through cloud. As you look upon the pearl, think about the certainty of the cycle of life, yet at the same time its fragility. Take into yourself the responsibility for guardianship of the cycle and this world. You should strive to protect it, as Solarisel protected the pearl, and as those who now attend him protect the hostling of the pearl.

The nine hienamas draw symbols of protection over the pearl and utter invocations of protective spirits. It is then given back to Solarisel. The dehar is placed upon a litter and carried away to another part of the Nayati where he will recover.

All in attendance now partake of a feast to celebrate the safe arrival of the pearl of potential. It, and its hostling, will be guarded with keen vigilance for the following two weeks, until the hatching at Natalia.

Spend some time communing with others at the feast. You may go to the inner sanctum and commune with Solarisel if you so wish.

When you are ready to conclude the visualisation, return to normal consciousness as usual.

Dismantle the Nayati in the usual way.

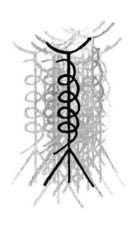

Brynie

The Path of the Brynilid

Now that the rehuna has familiarised themselves with the dehara and have performed majhahns to them, they begin to perform majhahns for specific effects. Brynie incorporates new dehara, who have been created for specialised workings. The rehuna learns how to create their own dehara. With this path comes the confidence and experience to command the dehara specifically. Self knowledge can be taken further by performing majhahns to the dehara asking for help in this regard.

The Symbol Brynie

Brynie symbolises awareness of the self and of the environment. It represents the balancing of different aspects within the self, and the deflection of harm through that awareness. This symbol is also used as a 'grounding' symbol, in conjunction with Ara and Neoma. As the rehuna's meditations become more intense, it is important they use this symbol. It can be drawn on the forehead, either with paint or with scented oil.

The symbol is drawn by beginning at the top, working downwards, and adding the spiral last. The name should be chanted three times as it's drawn.

As with the previous two symbols, the rehuna should spend time learning the symbol and familiarising themselves with it. They should practice combining it with agmara and the other symbols and use it during dehara meditations.

It can now be used in any majhahn or arojhahn, after Neoma has been drawn. At the centre of the Nayati, the rehuna should draw Brynie in the air before them, and/or upon the forehead, and say: 'Brynie, be the axis of grounding.'

Brynie Initiation

By this time, the rehuna will have consolidated a relationship with their hienama guide. The initiation majhahn into Brynie should incorporate as much personal imagery as possible. The rehuna now knows the process and should do what they feel is appropriate.

Deharan Majhahn

Majhahn is used for several different purposes. In Dehara, it is used to explore visualised realms and to commune with the dehara native to those realms; to affect reality to acquire a desired result; to search for self-knowledge. The rehuna may approach the dehara for making positive changes. In Neoma, the rehuna entered the realms of the dehara and communed with them. Now the dehara will be invoked directly into the Nayati. The rehuna will become familiar with their presence, before progressing to majhahns for specific effects.

For workings that involve the invocation of a dehar into the centre of the Nayati, the rehuna will invoke elemental dehara vegrandis into the quarters, and Aghama into the centre. They may also create a Halo of Power (magical circle) as extra protection. Otherwise the creation of the Nayati is the same as usual.

Elemental Dehara

When the rehuna performs majhahn to, for example, Aruhani, it would not be appropriate to acknowledge him in the north quarter as well. His energy should be focused in the centre of the Nayati for the work in hand.

Therefore, the rehuna uses alternative quarter entities for certain majhahns involving the dehara. These are dehara vegrandis that pertain to the compass directions and the elements. Their status can be seen as just below that of Aruhani and the other major dehara. They act as gate guardians for their quarters, and messengers of the dehara who reside in those realms. Like the major dehara, the elemental entities are tall and commanding androgynous presences.

North: Phorlakh

 This is the sign of Phorlakh who is the elemental guardian of the north. His element is earth, his season is winter and his time of day is midnight. Phorlakh is ruler of all creatures of the north, including bulls and minotaurs, dragons who dwell within caves, basilisks, gargoyles and

centaurs. His sacred animal is the forest wolf.

Phorlakh wears a coat of leaves and flowers. His hair is nut brown and braided with tasselled grasses. He exudes a perfume of loamy earth and the rich scents of the deepwoods. His skin is dark brown, his eyes black.

Phorlakh is attended by elementals, known as Fholids. These are creatures of earth, who may manifest as entities comprised of twigs and leaves, or they may simply be glimpsed as glowing eyes in the dark of the forest, blending with the natural environment so they are mostly invisible. They also manifest as beautiful green and brown skinned hara, whose hair is like leaves and moss. Their fingernails might be poisoned. Although tricky by nature, Fholids can be appeased with gifts of sparkling things, and may then be set as elemental guardians over property.

The Sign of Oorn

The palace of Phorlakh is Oorn, a gigantic tree in the centre of the mythical Forest of Ijhimere. It is a representation of the World Tree, which is also a symbol of Aruhani. Entrance to Aruhani's inner realm may be made through the roots of Oorn.

East: Naivedya

Naivedya is the elemental guardian of the east. His element is air, his season is spring and his time of day is dawn. Naivedya is ruler of all creatures of the east, including winged steeds, flying dragons of the mountains, magical birds, gryphons and cockatrices. His sacred animal is the peacock.

 In appearance, Naivedya is tall and thin, with a pale gold cast to his skin. His eyes are a deep yellow. Occasionally, he manifests as winged, but can fly without or without wings. He wears a robe of pale feathers, decorated at the hem with peacock feathers. His pale floating hair is also braided with feathers.

The elemental beings under Naivedya's control are the Pazini. These are flighty, sylph-like creatures, who move very quickly. They sometimes manifest as beautiful golden hara who can dissolve into the air or transform into a flock of birds in an instant. Pazini can cause confusion and lead the unsuspecting into high and rarefied places, where the air is thin and strange sights may be glimpsed. They congregate on rooftops and ride the winds. If given the proper offerings of perfume, they can be commanded to call up winds, even to create hurricanes.

The Sign of Shuraya

Naivedya's palace, Shuraya, is found at the summit of the Shadowpeak, a mountain at the heart of the world. It has no roof, being open to the winds and is comprised of many twisting columns that can appear to be natural rock formations. The path to Shuraya is steep and narrow, and lined with invisible wind harps, the music of which can beguile and confuse the unwary traveller. Entrance to Miyacala's realm can be made from the most central point of Shuraya. The portal is a spinning vortex of air.

South: Elauria

 This is the sign of Elauria, who is the elemental guardian of the south. His element is fire, his season is summer and his time of day is noon. Elauria is ruler of all creatures of the south, including firedrakes, salamanders, firefoxes, manticores and the phoenix. His sacred animal is the lion.

Elauria wears splendid robes of crimson, gold and orange. His hair is a mass of flames and his eyes are burning red. If he is caught and held for more than three minutes, which is very difficult, since he is extremely hot, he changes into a form less dangerous and may be safely touched. In this form, he takes the shape of a red-haired har. Elauria can impart many gifts to those brave enough to risk his blaze. He bestows passion and conviction, and can fan the flames of love.

The attendants of Elauria are the Flimmerids, who bask in pools of fire. These are the elementals who manifest as streaks of smoke and a smell of burning. If they should manifest as hara, they are, like their ruler, seen as having bright red hair. Flimmerids are the least easily appeased of all the elemental creatures. Even if they consent to assist a rehuna, they might forget their purpose or get bored, and then cause damage.

The Sign of Auracas

The Palace of Flame is Auracas, located in a burning desert. Fires burn in every cavernous chamber, and lick across the searing walls. Jewels are formed in the heart of Auracas, which may be taken by the intrepid visitor. Access to Agave's

132

realm is through a pit in the throne room of Elauria.

West: Harudha

This is the sign of Harudha, who is the elemental guardian of the west. His element is water, his season is autumn and his time of day is evening. Harudha is ruler of all creatures of the west, including wyverns, sea serpents, lamias, hippocamps, and hydras. His sacred animal is the serpent.

Harudha appears as a sinuous blue or green skinned hair with extremely long waving hair, as if it is moving underwater. Sometimes, his skin may be scaled like that of a serpent. If he is clothed, it might appear that his garments are comprised of water droplets, like dew upon a spider's web. He might also appear clad in garments made entirely of pearls. He brings with him a sense of freshness as of cool clear water, and his presence does much to refresh and restore tired senses. As a dehar of water, he is concerned with emotions and psychism.

The elementals of the water realm are the Shaddari. Sometimes these manifest as creatures with the upper bodies of beautiful hara and the lower bodies of snakes or eels. Their appearance might also be that of a mer-har with a fish's tail. These elementals congregate in isolated coves, or else in the pools of mountain falls, and other unfrequented spots. Here, they like to sing. Shaddari can sing to the soul, and their siren voices may soothe or inflame, depending on their whim and whether they have been appeased with gifts of food and drink.

The Sign of Fayganza

133

The Palace of Water is Fayganza, found deep in the Lake of Endless Sighs. It is a huge, half ruined cyclopean edifice, as if built by an ancient and forgotten race. The realm of Lunil may be accessed from this place by entering a huge whirling vortex at the centre of the palace.

Experiencing the Elemental Dehara

Before invoking the elemental dehara vegrandis into a Nayati, the rehuna should spend some time meditating on each of the elemental realms. They should visit each Palace as described above, and establish a relationship with the presiding dehar and his attendants.

Invoking the Elemental Dehara Vegrandis

The rehuna should speak clearly, and visualise the dehar at each quarter as they invoke him. For ruhahn, the invocations may be changed to include plural personal pronouns rather than singular.

The rehuna goes to the north, draws the sign of Phorlakh, raises arms and commands:

> In this quarter, I call upon Phorlakh, dehar of Earth,
> Who reigns in the North,
> To be present in this Nayati
> And to witness this majhahn.
> Phorlakh, instil within me the power of Earth,
> Stand and protect me in the North,
> In the name of the fifth element,
> Aghama, the star and your master.

The rehuna should draw Ara in the air before them. They should then bow to the dehar and visualise that he bows to them also.

134

The rehuna then goes to the East, draws the sign of Naivedya, raises arms and commands:

> *In this quarter, I call upon Naivedya, dehar of Air,*
> *Who reigns in the East,*
> *To be present in this Nayati*
> *And to witness this majhahn.*
> *Naivedya, instil within me the power of Air,*
> *Stand and protect me in the East,*
> *In the name of the fifth element,*
> *Aghama, the star and your master.*

The rehuna should draw Ara in the air before them. They should then bow to the dehar and visualise that he bows to them also.

The rehuna then goes to the South, draws the sign of Elauria, raises arms and commands:

> *In this quarter, I call upon Elauria, dehar of Fire,*
> *Who reigns in the South,*
> *To be present in this Nayati*
> *And to witness this majhahn.*
> *Elauria, instil within me the power of Fire,*
> *Stand and protect me in the South,*
> *In the name of the fifth element,*
> *Aghama, the star and your master.*

The rehuna should draw Ara in the air before them. They should then bow to the dehar and visualise that he bows to them also.

The rehuna then goes to the West, draw the sign of Harudha, raises arms and commands:

> *In this quarter, I call upon Harudha, dehar of Water,*
> *Who reigns in the West,*
> *To be present in this Nayati*
> *And to witness this majhahn.*
> *Harudha, instil within me the power of Water,*
> *Stand and protect me in the West,*
> *In the name of the fifth element,*
> *Aghama, the star and your master.*

The rehuna should draw Ara in the air before them. They should then bow to the dehar and visualise that he bows to them also.

In the centre of the Nayati, the rehuna draws the sign of the Aghama, raises their arms and commands:

> *'In the centre, the cauldron of creation*
> *I call to Aghama, light of all,*
> *Tigron of the Spheres,*
> *To be present here in this Nayati,*
> *Astale Aghama, be with me now!*
> *Protect and empower me!'*

The rehuna should bow to the dehar, and visualise him bowing to them.

Dismantling the Elemental Nayati

As they speak the closing words, the rehuna should focus on feeling that connection with each realm being severed. In each quarter, after the closing has been performed, mundane reality returns.

The rehuna goes to the north, raises arms, and commands:

> *Phorlakh, Dehar of the Elemental North,*
> *Your presence here is always welcome.*
> *I release you from this Nayati*
> *Travel as you will*
> *In this world and all others,*
> *Until our paths cross again,*
> *In the name of the fifth element,*
> *Aghama, the star and your master,*
> *I bid you farewell.*

Ara is drawn in reverse.

The rehuna goes to the east and commands:

> *Naivedya, Dehar of the Elemental East,*
> *Your presence here is always welcome.*
> *I release you from this Nayati*
> *Travel as you will*
> *In this world and all others,*
> *Until our paths cross again,*
> *In the name of the fifth element,*
> *Aghama, the star and your master,*
> *I bid you farewell.*

Ara is drawn in reverse

The rehuna goes to the south and commands:

> *Elauria, Dehar of the Elemental South*
> *Your presence here is always welcome.*
> *I release you from this Nayati*
> *Travel as you will*
> *In this world and all others,*
> *Until our paths cross again,*
> *In the name of the fifth element,*
> *Aghama, the star and your master,*
> *I bid you farewell.*

Ara is drawn in reverse

The rehuna goes to the west and commands:

> *Harudha, Dehar of the Elemental West,*
> *Your presence here is always welcome.*
> *I release you from this Nayati*
> *Travel as you will*
> *In this world and all others,*
> *Until our paths cross again,*
> *In the name of the fifth element,*
> *Aghama, the star and your master,*
> *I bid you farewell.*

Ara is drawn in reverse

In the centre, rehuna raises arms and says:

> *'Aghama, your presence here is always welcome,*
> *I release you from this Nayati*
> *Travel as you will*
> *In this world and all others,*
> *Until our paths cross again,*
> *I bid you farewell.'*

Ara is drawn, large, in reverse in the centre.

Now the rehuna directs the agmara energy back to the centre of creation. It is imagined that the rehuna and the space they occupy become their usual mundane selves. Thus, the Nayati is dismantled.

Equipment for Dehara Majhahn

For each working that follows, the rehuna may incorporate tools described in the introduction:

> Shayyai
> Vakei
> Incense
> Suitable music (Some examples are given in the appendices, but the rehuna may choose whatever they find appropriate and evocative.)

If the rehuna lacks any of the suggested equipment, they may improvise. For example, candles can be used instead of shayyai.

Preparation for Dehara Majhahn

The rehuna should station the shayyai bowls at each corner of the altar, if one is being used. Otherwise, the shayyai should be arranged about the room, (or open space, if outdoors), at each cardinal point. They should not be filled yet with any evaporating substance or lit.

Other personal items may be placed on the altar – artefacts of personal power or meaning, flowers, stones, carvings. If the rehuna possesses a statue or picture to represent the presiding dehar, it can be used as a centrepiece.

The rehuna may draw or paint Ara, Neoma and Brynie on the skin, if they so wish.

The room should be darkened, having only soft lighting, which will be extinguished once the shayyai are lit.

Aruhani Majhahn

The majhahn commences in the usual way by calling upon agmara, transforming into the visualised harish self, and drawing Ara and Neoma in the centre of the Nayati. Brynie may be drawn upon the forehead in scented oil or water.

Halo of Power

Because this is a working rather than a questing majhahn or seasonal arojhahn, the rehuna may create a Halo of Power as extra protection and containment. This is visualised as a circle of vibrating agmara that nothing can breach, unless with the rehuna's express permission and will.

The rehuna takes up the vakei and visualises strongly agmara emanating from its tip. They should draw a circle clockwise in the majhahn space and say:

> 'Halo of Agmara, protect me,
> Beyond, above, below and through all realms of
> time and space.
> Let no harm come to me.
> I am in here in good faith and good heart.
> In the name of the fifth element, Aghama, who is spirit.'

Nayati Invocations

To finish constructing the Nayati, the rehuna first invokes the elemental dehara vegrandis, and then calls Aghama into the centre.

The rehuna then fills and lights the shayyai and extinguishes all other light. Depending on the size of the bowls being used, the shayyai will burn for a few minutes, while Aruhani is invoked. The rehuna should experiment with measures, so that when they go into the meditation, eventually they will be in utter blackness.

Invoke Aruhani

The rehuna stands in the centre of the Nayati, draws the sign of Aruhani, visualises the dehar appearing, and says:

> *'Aruhani, Dehar of the Mysteries of Aruna, Life and Death*
> *I invite you into my presence*
> *Be with me and give to me knowledge*
> *of your realm and your being*
> *Let me walk the path to the dehara*
> *in the infinite reaches of the cosmos*
> *Ara is the gateway, Neoma the shield*
> *Brynie the axis.*
> *I call upon you, Dark One.*
> *Be with me now.'*

The rehuna stands for a few moments, breathing deeply, visualising the dehar, then draws the symbol of Aruhani, large, in the air before them. They invoke him using the chanted phrase:

> *'Astale Aruhani!'*

The rehuna releases the energy when it's appropriate, and welcomes Aruhani into the Nayati.

Visualisation:

Lie or sit comfortably. Close your eyes and breathe deeply for some moments.

See the elemental dehara standing at the portals in their quarters. Go now to the north and ask Phorlakh for permission to enter his realm. Give to him the sign of his

142

palace of Oorn.

Find yourself in a dark place, in the centre of the palace of
Oorn. There are steps before you, leading downwards into a
black hole. Descend these steps.

When you reach the bottom, your eyes gradually adjust to the
dim light. There is a portal before you. Draw upon it in
agmara light the sign of Julangis, Aruhani's Nayati. The portal
opens to you.
     You see that you are in an immense black Nayati. Bitter
incense fills the air and you sense unseen movement in the
shadows around you.
     Slowly, you become aware of a massive statue of Aruhani
ahead of you. Low lights burn around it.
     You feel unsafe and unsure. This is an initiatory
experience, and in some ways involves facing your fears. In
the distance, you hear strange booming sounds and cries, as if
other things are going on within this vast building that you
cannot see.

Go towards the statue. As you do so, it begins to glow with
red light. It is becoming transparent.
     Run forward and leap through the statue itself. As you do
so, you transform into a winged creature. You are leaping into
another realm, the abyss, the place of the unseen, of initiation.
This is the place to test your strength and your resolve.

You find yourself rushing through a vortex. You have no
physical body: you are simply a ball of energy. At first, there
is only blackness, but then lights appear ahead and you are
flying towards them fast. Bizarre and exotic images flash past
your mind's eye: cyclopean cities of obsidian stone,
impenetrable abysses, endless oceans of liquid metal, and
many other impossible sights.

Then, the strange scenes are past you, and you are flying
through a sepia darkness towards a beautiful golden light. As
you draw nearer, you see a new landscape. It is beautiful but

strange. In some ways it is stark, nothing more than barren black rocks and cliffs, but the pure buttery radiance around you transforms it. You see an enormous stepped pyramid ahead of you, and here you land upon the platform at its summit.

In the centre of the platform is a square opening in the floor, where you see steps leading downward. Then begin to descend the steps. The black walls on either side are veined with dark red light. The air is warm and smells of cloves and frankincense. You have entered the temple of Aruhani.

At the bottom of the steps, the dehar awaits you in a garden. Even though it's in the centre of the pyramid, it seems to be open to the air. The garden is the most peculiar you have ever seen. The plants are of the darkest hues: indigo, black and crimson. Fleshy flowers, the size of cartwheels, exude a perfume of jasmine and rot. Thorned vines snake across the black earth beneath your feet, writhing like serpents.

Aruhani sits cross-legged upon an altar of jet. He is of normal harish size: a beautiful creature with black skin, whose only garment is his abundant braided hair that covers him like a shawl. The soles of his feet are dyed red with ochre. His power is primal and unnerving. He is the harish equivalent of the darkest of the mother goddesses of ancient human cultures. He has the capacity to be terrifying and destructive, but he also has the capacity for the greatest love and compassion.

Face Aruhani without fear. Tell him why you are there, what you wish to learn; about magic, the world, and about yourself. He might take you to a different place, or offer you a gift of some kind.

When you feel ready to return to normal consciousness, become aware of your physical body where it is sitting/lying. Move your fingers and toes to ground yourself. Imagine the Nayati as it really is around you. Breathe deep and be conscious of the air going in and out of your lungs. When you feel ready, open your eyes.

The rehuna now lights candles or turns on a soft-light lamp to dismantle the Nayati.

The rehuna stands in the centre, raises arms and says:

> *'Aruhani, Dehar of Aruna, Life and Death*
> *Your presence here is always welcome.*
> *I release you from this Nayati*
> *Travel as you will*
> *In this world and all others,*
> *Until our paths cross again,*
> *In the name of the fifth element,*
> *Aghama, the star and your master,*
> *I bid you farewell.'*

The Nayati is then dismantled in the usual manner.

Miyacala Majhahn

Miyacala is essentially concerned with magical and self knowledge, rites of passage and initiation and learning. He is also connected with inspiration and creativity. Although his eyes are blind, he sees better than most, because he uses his inner eyes to perceive all. Therefore, the rehuna may also approach him for insight into situations and ask him to reveal information they require.

In this majhahn, the rehuna will visit Miyacala's Temple of Ascension. This is the ultimate Nayati of initiation.

The rehuna creates the Nayati in the same manner they created it for the previous majhahn.

The shayyai are lit and all other lights extinguished.

Invoke Miyacala

The rehuna stands in the centre of the Nayati, draws the sign of Miyacala upon the air, raises their arms, and commands:

> 'Miyacala, Dehar of Initiation, Knowledge and Inspiration
> I invite you into my presence
> Be with me and give to me knowledge of your realm
> and your being
> Let me walk the path to the dehara
> in the infinite reaches of the cosmos
> Ara is the gateway, Neoma the shield, Brynie the axis,
> I call upon you, Dehar of Ultimate Perception,
> Be with me now.'

The rehuna stands for a few moments, breathing deeply, visualising the dehar. They then draw Miyacala's symbol in the air before them, and invoke him with the chant:

'*Astale Miyacala*'.

The rehuna releases the energy when it's appropriate, and welcomes Miyacala into the Nayati.

The Visualisation

Sit or lie down facing the east. See Naivedya in the eastern portal, and rise up from your body to approach him. Ask for permission to enter the eastern realm and give to him the sign of his palace Fayganza. Proceed through Naivedya's temple to the centre, where a rushing vortex of air provides access to Tahanica, Miyacala's Nayati.

As you stand before the vortex, draw the symbol of Tahanica in the air before you. Step through the vortex.

You find yourself in a place of radiant light. It is an enormous Nayati, where everything is white or silver. Although the light is so bright that it's difficult to see things clearly, you perceive there are fountains here, not of water but of sparkling radiance. Columns of swirling brightness run down both sides of the temple, and between them you can see tall tripods, upon which sacred flames burn.

At the far end of the temple is a flight of steps, at the top of which is an altar. You are drawn to ascend these steps.

At the top, you stand before the altar, which is a simple cube of white marble. Veins within the stone glow with sparkling light. Miyacala appears to you, stepping out of the radiance around him to become visible to your eyes. He is tall and robed in white, his long white hair hanging to his waist. His eyes are blind, but upon his brow is a radiant star, signifying his great inner sight. You are aware that he can see right into you, to your darkest corners, your deepest secrets. Before Miyacala, you can conceal nothing.

Ask him now to assist you in your journey to self-knowledge, into whatever dark and dangerous corners that might take you. Tell him of your visits to his brethren, Aruhani, Lunil and Agave, and ask that he might reveal further knowledge to you. Ask that you might walk into your own place of shadows, the place where your demons lurk. You wish to begin unmasking them and banishing them from your life. Ask Miyacala this in honesty. If you have any hesitation or doubt, you should not yet undertake this journey.

If Miyacala is receptive to your request, he raises his hand, upon which another star burns. Raise your own hand in response and press it to his. You will receive in this way his guiding light for your journey, which will blaze before you like a torch, banishing shadows.

When you draw your hand away from that of the dehar, you see that a star burns there also.

Miyacala now commands the altar to move, and it slowly swings to the side. You see that beneath it is a flight of steps going downwards into darkness. This is the path you must take. It is the realm of the mind, of thought and memory. On this occasion, you will perhaps not venture very far, but your task is to illuminate this dark realm, to face its demons and transform them with your light. Go now into the darkness. Miyacala will walk with you.

What follows will be personal to you, and you cannot be given instruction as to what you will see and experience, but Miyacala and his penetrating light is with you, keeping you safe.

When you are ready to return, Miyacala will take you back to his Nayati. From there, return to normal reality.

The rehuna should ensure they ground themselves thoroughly after this meditation, as it can cause disorientation.

The rehuna should light candles or turn on a soft-light lamp and dismantle the Nayati.

The rehuna stands in the centre, raises arms and says:

> *'Miyacala, Dehar of Knowledge and Initiation,*
> *I honour you for the teaching you have imparted.*
> *I release you from this Nayati*
> *Travel as you will*
> *In this world and all others,*
> *Until our paths cross again,*
> *In the name of the fifth element,*
> *Aghama, the star and your master,*
> *I bid you farewell.'*

The Nayati is then dismantled in the usual manner.

Agave Majhahn

This majhahn may be used at times when the rehuna is experiencing psychological or physical discomfort, or they wish to work in majhahn for some other who is experiencing these things.

The rehuna creates the Nayati in the same manner they created it for the previous majhahn.

The shayyai are lit and all other lights extinguished.

Invoke Agave

The rehuna sits in the centre of the Nayati, facing south. They should breathe deeply with closed eyes, visualising Agave. The symbol of Agave is drawn in the air. The rehuna says:

> 'Astale Agave!
> You of the fire, the He and She in One,
> Protector, warrior, and healer
> Aid me in my time of need.
> I come to you in pain,
> I come to you in hope.
> Ease my pain, strengthen my hope.
> Astale Agave!
> In the fall, you are the destroyer,
> Harbinger of the winter, harbinger of the need to rejuvenate.
> With your spear you destroy all.

You set fire to life, bringing death
But within death is life.
In your fire is the seed of creativity.
Even as you destroy, you bury the seeds
That will sprout from the snow and bring spring to the land.
Agave, in the spring, you are the harbinger of life,
Stirring the fires of lust and love,
Stirring the need to live.
Astale Agave!
You are the promise of creativity,
Of inspiration, of warmth restored to the land.
Agave the healer, Agave the protector, Agave the warrior,
I call to you to lead me to fall, to lead me to spring.
I call you to spark the fire within my soul.
Astale Agave!'

(The last line is repeated to raise power.)

The rehuna releases the energy when it's appropriate, and welcomes Agave into the Nayati.

Now, the rehuna lights a flame (shayya or candle) and some incense and places it in the south. They should anoint themselves with Dragon's Blood oil, or paint Agave's symbol sigil in red/orange on the chest.

The Visualisation

Sit in the centre of the Nayati and face the flame you lit. Stare into this flame, and see a doorway of fire within it.

Now, visualise stepping into that door way. Do not fear the flames. They will not hurt you.

Once you have passed through the flame door, you come to a field. It is the site of a recent battle. You see Agave walking in the field. Every so often, he kneels and heals a har or slays him, depending on the nature of his wounds. Agave heals or slays from compassion. Some can be healed, some are too hurt. He looks over at you. Tell him why you are here. From there let the meditation take you where it will.

The rehuna should light candles or turn on a soft-light lamp and dismantle the Nayati.

The rehuna stands in the centre, raises arms and says:

> *'Agave, Dehar of the Sacred Fire*
> *Protector, Warrior and Healer,*
> *I honour you for the teaching you have imparted.*
> *I entered this Nayati in pain and without hope.*
> *I leave it now with hope renewed and pain banished.*
> *I revere you, Agave, for bringing me strength.'*

The Nayati is then dismantled in the usual manner.

Lunil Majhahn

This majhahn to Lunil invokes him into the Nayati, in the same way Aruhani was invoked Aruhani in the previous majhahn.

The rehuna creates the Nayati in the same manner they created it for the previous majhahn.

The shayyai are lit and all other lights extinguished.

Invoke Lunil

The rehuna stand in the centre of the Nayati, facing west, draws the sign of Lunil, visualises the dehar and says:

> *Lunil, Dehar of the Mysteries of the Moon and of Magic*
> *I invite you into my presence*
> *Be with me and give to me knowledge*
> *of your realm and your being*
> *Let me walk the path to the dehara*
> *in the infinite reaches of the cosmos*
> *Ara is the gateway, Neoma the shield, Brynie the axis,*
> *I call upon you, Dehar of Silver Light,*
> *Be with me now.'*

The rehuna stands for a few moments, breathing deeply, visualising the dehar, then draws Lunil's symbol in the air before them. Lunil is invoked using the chanted phrase:

'Astale Lunil!'

The rehuna releases the energy when it's appropriate, and welcomes Lunil into the Nayati.

Visualisation

Lie or sit comfortably. Close your eyes and breathe deeply for some moments.

See the elemental dehara standing at the portals in their quarters. Go now to the west and ask Harudha for permission to enter his realm. Give to him the sign for his palace Shuraya.

Enter through the western portal, into the Palace of Water. Proceed to the centre of this edifice and dive into the vortex you find there.

You emerge into a realm of silver, white and blue of many different hues and qualities. This is the quarter of elemental flux, of the building blocks of magic.

Your feet lead you to Loraylah, the Nayati of Lunil, which is a shining edifice of shifting elements. Before you enter it, draw the symbol of Loraylah in the air before you.

The chambers of this Nayati have a wavering, nebulous quality. You walk through fountains and cascades of light and energy. You walk through pools of shining ether, where strange creatures flash and shimmer beneath the surface. This is a realm of mutability. It embodies the quicksilver aspects of your being; flashes of creative inspiration, the strong and sometimes turbulent currents of emotion.

In the inner sanctum, the central chamber, of this Nayati, Lunil is enthroned. He is a beautiful blue-skinned creature, whose eyes are violet and seem to contain absolute knowledge of your innermost self. He is not judgmental.

Though he sees all, he embodies compassion and understanding. You are drawn to him.

Before the dehar's throne, is a circular pool, which contains the magical waters of Forgetfulness and Remembrance. Next to the pool is a silver cup on a chain. Lunil gestures for you to drink from the pool. It is up to you whether you choose to remember or to forget. Whatever the case, the fluid is healing and enlightening. As you drink it, it cools your being and soothes your mind. See what images it brings to you, what lessons might be learned from the waters.

Now spend some time exploring this realm, and if you wish to, ask Lunil to walk with you there. If there is anything you particularly want to see or learn, ask for these things to be shown to you.

When you feel ready to return to normal consciousness, become aware of your physical body where it is sitting/lying. Move your fingers and toes to ground yourself. Imagine the Nayati as it really is around you. Breathe deep and be conscious of the air going in and out of your lungs. When you feel ready, open your eyes.

The rehuna should light candles or turn on a soft-light lamp and dismantle the Nayati.

The rehuna stands in the centre, raises arms and says:

> 'Lunil, Dehar of the Moon and of Magic,
> Your presence here is always welcome.
> I release you from this Nayati
> Travel as you will
> In this world and all others,
> Until our paths cross again,
> In the name of the fifth element,
> Aghama, the star and your master,
> I bid you farewell.'

The Nayati is then dismantled in the usual manner.

Aghama Majhahn

The Aghama is a very powerful being, who can control reality through the forces of the imagination. He can move through time-space and alter time-space for others. In a sense, like a star, he is an immense gravity well. Gravity, in science, alters time and space, creating among other things the non-linear nature of reality with its wide range of possibilities. This is why this is a majhahn to the sun and the stars. Stars represent balance and an essential part of the DNA of the universe. They serve as maintainers of the webs of reality, of energy, of imagination.

In this majhahn, the rehuna not only gains knowledge of the Aghama but also harnesses the energies of imagination as it becomes reality and visa versa. They should receive an enormous power/creativity boost. By working with the Aghama and the stars, they will also channel that energy into themselves, to such an extent that they will become a living amplifier of it. They might find that the concepts of space and time merge into one, and that time becomes non-linear, leading them down roads that will enable them to begin exploring how to 'walk' across time, and how to be extremely aware of possibilities.

The music for this majhahn should be something ambient and dark. The rehuna should paint or draw all symbols associated with the majhahn on their skin.

Prior to this majhahn, the rehuna should undergo purification, by taking a bath or a shower. This should be done with intention and followed by exercise, such as yoga or tai chi. These procedures serve as a warm-up for the actual majhahn.

First, the rehuna should create a sigil to represent the Aghama and the working. It should be a symbol derived solely from the rehuna's imagination and should be painted over the heart in red pigment.

As the rehuna paints the sigil, they should say the following:

> 'Aghama, lord of time-space,
> Brightest star that shines above and within me,
> Take me to the heart of the universe,
> Open me to the secrets of time-space,
> Of imagination that turns into reality,
> Of reality that turns into imagination,
> Open me to the essence of the universe,
> To the manifestation of possibilities,
> The awareness of all realities,
> Take me to the web of power, Oh Aghama,
> And through it help me to know myself,
> Not merely as a being of flesh and blood,
> But also of imagination and reality,
> Of time and space.
> Help me to balance myself,
> Within imagination and reality
> Give me serenity and love,
> Intelligence and will
> Let me find and know myself
> In all realities, in all imaginations, in space and in time,
> Show me the way to the web of power,
> The creation helix of the universe,
> Cauldron of being.
> Astale Aghama!"

The rehuna should now sit for some moments, visualising

agmara streaming down into their body, filling the symbol over their heart, bringing with it awareness and sensitivity to the most subtle energies.

Then, the rehuna draws or paints the symbol in red, on a piece of paper and lays it in front of them. They should prepare for meditation.

The Visualisation:

At first, you find yourself travelling along a red cord of power. You see before you a door comprised of the sigil. Open the door and step through. You see the fundamental essence of the universe: planets and stars forming a DNA spiral.

Follow the red cord to our star, the sun. Within the sun, you will find the Aghama, a creature of incredible brilliance and power, his beauty so raw and primal it is almost painful to behold. His eyes are closed, but he becomes aware of your presence and gazes upon you. Then he stretches out one hand to you. Take it without fear.

You feel a wave of power surge through you. It may feel strange and a little terrifying but let it flow through your body. The Aghama steps out of the sun and takes you on a journey. He shows to you the universe and how the energy of it is formed, how time-space-imagination-reality work both within and without you. You go to the centre of the universe, the cauldron of creation where stars are born. In this place, you can experience understanding of reality, if only in fleeting glimpses.

Spend some time here, letting your mind wander where it will. Commune with the Aghama in whatever way feels right to you. Go into the past and the future. Dream up new realities. Become a star.

When you are ready to conclude the meditation, the Aghama takes you to a portal, comprised of the sigil you drew over

162

your heart and on the paper beside you in physical reality. You pass through this doorway back to your body.

When the rehuna opens their eyes, they should take up the sigil drawing and infuse it with their essence, either through intention, the breath or whatever method feels right to them. Finally, they should take the sigil drawing and burn it, saying:

> *'Aghama, lord of time-space-imagination-reality,*
> *I offer to you this essence of mine mixed with yours.*
> *Take it as an offering and as appreciation for your gifts to me.*
> *I release you from this Nayati*
> *Travel as you will*
> *In this world and all others,*
> *Until our paths cross again,*
> *I bid you farewell.'*

Ara is drawn, large, in reverse in the centre.

The rehuna then releases the dehara vegrandis from the elemental quarters.

The rehuna directs the agmara energy back to the centre of creation. It is imagined that the rehuna and the space they occupy become their usual mundane selves.

Enchantments and Hexes: the Practice of Magari

A magari is an action to achieve a specific result, with intention, whether that's the skewering of a wax doll with a needle, the creation of an herbal sachet, writing symbols or words down on paper and then burning it, burning a candle of a particular colour, eating or drinking something the rehuna has imbued with intention, or whatever the imagination of the rehuna devises. Magaris are versatile because the rehuna can design their own, incorporating whatever tools, ingredients or actions they wish. The tools are used *with intention to achieve a particular result.*

The difference between a magari and a majhahn is that a majhahn incorporates the whole process of Nayati building, while the magari is the working performed within that Nayati. But magaris can also be performed any time, in any place.

A binding magari is given below as an example, but the most effective magaris are those the rehuna invents themselves.

To do this, the rehuna decides upon the focus of the magari, designs it, choosing whatever ingredients they desire, and then casts it within the Nayati. The rehuna may simply empower an object to do a specific job, which is then placed in a particular place. It can be programmed for how long the effect will last, by the rehuna intending this will be so as they work the magari.

Magaris and majhahns associated with growth and expansion should be performed in the waxing and full moon; banishings or bindings in the waning moon, or even in the dark of the moon, depending on the seriousness of the situation.

A Deharan Binding Magari

The magari should be performed in the waning or dark moon. It is designed to prevent another person from harming the rehuna. The purpose of this magari is to curtail someone's negative actions on the rehuna's life. It should not be performed with the purpose of causing harm.

First, the rehuna decides upon the focus of the magari, which is an object to represent the person they wish to bind. This is referred to as the talisman. It can be a drawing, a photograph or a fashioned representation of the object of the magari. The rehuna may write the person's name in a pattern on paper, or create a sigil of it. The rehuna may use some small item that belongs to the object of the magari and clippings of hair or nails. The rehuna should incorporate relevant herbs such as thistle or nettle. Symbols of the dehara may be incorporated. The rehuna may create a pouch containing several of the above mentioned items. They will also need a length of red ribbon to wind around the talisman multiple times.

To begin, the rehuna creates majhahn space in which to work, to their preferences.

The rehuna sets their equipment before them, and creates the talisman. When it is done, the rehuna either points at it with the vakei, or the first two fingers of their dominant hand and says:

'I name you (the name of the person in question).'

Now, the rehuna takes up the talisman and begins to wind the red ribbon around it, saying:

> *'I bind you in the name of Aruhani*
> *That your physical actions cannot touch me*
> *I bind you in the name of Miyacala*
> *That your thoughts cannot touch me*
> *I bind you in the name of Agave*
> *That your will cannot touch me*
> *I bind you in the name of Lunil*
> *That your feelings cannot touch me*
> *I bind you in the name of Aghama*
> *My protector and guardian*
> *Evil words against me are not believed*
> *Evil actions against me rebound*
> *Evil intentions against me dissipate into the ethers*
> *I am invisible to you*
> *I vanish from your thoughts and feelings*
> *You cannot touch me*
> *In the name of the dehara, this is so!*
> *You are bound (name)*
> *And have no power in my realm of being!'*

The rehuna holds the talisman for some time, investing it with their will. They should breathe agmara into it. The rehuna then raises power in their preferred manner and directs it into the talisman.

When it is done, the rehuna should put the enemy from their mind and let the magari do its work. The talisman should either be burned or buried.

Further Dehara Majhahns

As well as the major dehara and the elemental dehara vegrandis, other dehara have been created by rehunas during meditation and majhahn. Some of these were designed deliberately for a specific effect, while others evolved spontaneously. The last task of Brynie is for the rehuna to begin creating their own dehara, but prior to this instruction, examples are given of different majhahns that incorporate both the more familiar dehara as well as new dehara vegrandis.

The following Chamber of Gateways majhahn incorporates material that was received by a rehuna during meditation. It is used to explore the inner realms. Rehunas who are engaged in creative projects will find this majhahn useful, as it can be used to access any imaginary realm. The rehuna may then explore that realm in order to find inspired information.

Travelling the Otherlanes

The otherlanes are visualised spiritual paths that link different points in space and time. They can also be travelled to reach imaginary realms. A rehuna may create their own map of the otherlanes if they so wish, although their use is more prevalent in majhahn beyond Brynie. However, some instruction is given in their use during this level, in preparation for later journeys.

To access the otherlanes, the rehuna visualises a creature known as a sedu (plural: sedim). This appears in earthly reality as a magnificent horse, although that is not its true form. It is more properly a vehicle of energy that propels and protects the traveller as they negotiate the otherlanes. Sedim create and enter portals into these interdimensional highways.

The Chamber of Gateways Majhahn

During the visualisation in this majhahn, the rehuna visualises riding a sedu to another realm. They might receive impressions of its true form (for them) during the visualisation.

The rehuna creates their Nayati in the usual way, incorporating as much or as little of the procedures they have learned as they prefer.

Visualisation

Lie or sit comfortably and breathe deeply. See the dehara/dehara vegrandis hanging in their quarter portals.

Imagine that a portal to the otherlanes opens in the centre of the Nayati. It could be a vortex of energy or a portal of light. From it, a sedu manifests before you in the room. It is a massive beast and you can hear it breathing. This sedu will carry you to realms unseen. It is not a horse, but merely appears as one. The sedim are guardians of the ethers and will protect you on your journeys.

Mount the creature and see that the vortex of energy is enveloping you both, like an immense dark tornado. The sedu leaps up into its funnel and then you are travelling the otherlanes, the space between the worlds, between the layers of reality.

You are galloping through a void. There are no stars around you, but gradually you perceive a faint light up ahead. As you draw closer, you see that it is huge dark shape, surrounded by a silver nimbus. The shape resembles a spinning top in shape, or an old-fashioned Christmas bauble. It is an ellipsoid with its top and bottom drawn down into points. This is the Chamber of Gateways, the portal to many other realities.

You are so close now that the Chamber fills your entire vision. The sedu passes right through its walls and you find yourself enclosed by it.

The Chamber is entirely black. You can see no walls and no floor or ceiling. Your sedu hangs within it. Then, as you gaze around you, a black plinth emerges in the middle of the Chamber. It emits a faint silvery glow.

Dismount from the sedu. Although you cannot see a floor, you can walk upon it. Approach the plinth.

A huge book, like a grimoire, appears before you on the plinth. As you look at it, it opens of its own accord. The pages are entirely black. But even as you gaze at it, you see that silver writing appears and then disappears. Read what it says. This is a message for you alone. Spend some time examining the book, and any information that appears.

Now the plinth fades into the background. To see it, it's like looking at a faint star. You don't look directly at it to see it, but a little to the side.

Black mirrors appear on the walls around you, to each quarter. These are gateways to other realms, and to all corners of the Wraeththu world that has been dreamed into being by the minds of others. In the mirrors, you can see whatever you wish to see, and use them as portals to go wherever you wish, not just the imagined world of Wraeththu. The Chamber is the starting point of all such journeys, and you can visit it at any time, through a sedu.

Now, mount the sedu once more and ride off through one of the mirrors. Spend some time investigating this inner realm.

When you are ready, return to normal reality and ground yourself.

The rehuna then dismantles the Nayati in the usual way.

169

Aloyt Majhahn

Aloyt (pronounced al-oh-it) is a dehar of dreams, and this majhahn is again particularly useful for rehunas of a creative nature, since it can be used to acquire inspiration.

Aloyt is dark skinned, has long dread-locks, and his eyes are blue. The rehuna may invoke him to ask for dreams of a revealing nature. In order to commune with Aloyt, the rehuna invokes him into their dreams, so this majhahn does not require the creation of a Nayati. The rehuna performs it in bed, before going to sleep.

As part of the majhahn, the rehuna takes 100 deep breaths, in through the nose and out through the mouth, breathing down into the stomach. Taking, or even counting, 100 breaths might sound difficult, but if the rehuna should drift off to sleep before reaching the required amount, the majhahn will work just as effectively.

Before composing themselves for sleep, the rehuna chants the following:

> 'Aruhani as the Earth beneath my feet,
> Lunil as the guiding light for my spirit in the twilight lands,
> Agave as my fiery protector on paths unknown
> Miyacala as the clear memory so I won't forget this journey
> Aghama as the spirit to fire up my own spirit
> Aloyt, Dehar of Dreams, as the inspiration to creativity.'

The rehuna lies down in bed, flat on their back. They should visualise a flight of steps in front of them, leading upwards. They should take a deep breath through the nostrils and exhale through the mouth. This is done 100 times, with the rehuna imagining that they are climbing a step on each breath. In the process, they will energize themselves because they're enlivening the energy centres of their body.

The Sigil of Aloyt

The Visualisation:

At the hundredth breath, you come to a door with a symbol
on it, which is Aloyt's symbol. Open the door and enter into
the twilight lands. It's dark, but you can see twinkling lights.
You come to a stone Nayati upon a mountain. Inside the
Nayati is an altar, upon which stands an unlit lamp. Light the
altar lamp. The flame grows higher and higher until it goes
through the roof of the Nayati. Aloyt steps out of the shadows
made by the altar. He is dusky and very tall, with black dread
locks. His eyes are blue. He has a very powerful presence.
Talk with him for a time, and then allow yourself to drift off
to sleep. Dream and see what you remember the next day.

172

The Blood Majhahn of Agave

In times of dire need, or when a rehuna feels an exceptionally powerful majhahn is required, they can perform a blood rite. This is when the rehuna offers a little of their own blood to a dehar. As to why blood is given, as opposed to offerings such as food and drink, there are several reasons. Firstly, and most importantly, it is not a task to be undertaken lightly, so this lends gravity to the proceedings, which can focus the rehuna entirely on the majhahn itself. The rehuna might feel as if they are doing something difficult, which has great magical meaning. Also, blood is the fire and life of the body, for without it we cannot live. When a rehuna offers it, they offer some of their essence, which is a mark of trust. Finally, because rehunas would normally only undertake this kind of majhahn rarely, it marks the occasion as something set aside from normal magical work.

The rehuna does not have to offer a great deal of blood, just a very small amount. They should always take a small sample from the tip of a finger with an instrument that has been sterilised. This instrument should never be shared with another practitioner. The rehuna should not damage themselves.

For this majhahn, the rehuna should use both candles and shayyai. The Nayati should be filled with candles, because Agave appreciates their light. The shayyai should not be lit until later in the majhahn.

The Majhahn

The rehuna constructs their Nayati in the usual manner.

Invocation of Agave

The rehuna stands in the centre of the Nayati, draws the sign of Agave upon the air, raises their arms, and says:

> *'Astale Agave!*
> *I call you forth from the south*
> *Be with me now in spirit and body*
> *Agave of the fires, Agave of the spear and sword,*
> *Agave of the shield, Agave of the healing flame,*
> *Come to me and breathe into me your fiery spirit.*
> *I call you to spark the fires within my soul.*
> *Hear my petition, be my warrior in the world.*
> *Grant my desires without harm.*

The rehuna then chants and raises power:

> *'Astale, Agave'*

The Offering

After Agave is invoked, the rehuna goes to the altar and either silently or aloud speaks their desire to the dehar.

They say also: 'I offer my essence unto you. I offer from the fire of my body, that this may be so.'

The rehuna then makes their offering, which should be placed onto the burning charcoal of the incense.

The rehuna lights the shayyai.

The Visualisation

For this majhahn, the rehuna simply composes themselves for trance and goes where they will in the inner world, to commune with Agave, returning to normal consciousness when they are ready.

The rehuna should now drink a measure of red wine in Agave's honour.

Dismantling the Nayati

> 'Agave, Dehar of the Sacred Fire
> Protector, warrior, and healer,
> I honour your flame and your spirit.
> I release you from this Nayati
> Travel as you will
> In this world and all others,
> Until our paths cross again,
> I bid you farewell.'

Ara is drawn, large, in reverse in the centre.

The Nayati is then dismantled in the usual manner.

Lunil Majhahn of Ignizil

This majhahn incorporates Lunil's frequency of Agmara energy, which is known as Ignizil. A glass or goblet of water should be provided for each rehuna participating.

The Nayati is created in the usual way. The shayyai should be lit and all other light extinguished.

Invoke Lunil

Place a glass of water for each rehuna present in the centre of the Nayati. If more than one rehuna is doing this, the ruhahn should stand around the glasses with joined hands.

The rehuna concentrates once again on the image of Agmara cascading down from the centre of the universe as a greenish white light.

The rehuna draws the symbol for Ignizil in the air before them, or in their mind, and sees the ray of light change colour to a shade of blue.

Now the rehuna visualises Lunil, and says:

> *'Lunil, Blue Flame,*
> *Dehar of the Mysteries of the Moon and of Magic,*
> *who is of the night*
> *I invite you into this Nayati*
> *Be with me and give to me knowledge*
> *of your realm and your being*
> *Let me walk the path to the dehara*
> *in the infinite reaches of the cosmos*
> *Ara is the gateway, Neoma the shield, Brynie the axis,*
> *I call upon you, Dehar of Azure Light, be with me now!'*

The rehuna raises power: *'Astale Lunil'*

The Working

The rehuna should feel the dehar manifest in the middle of the Nayati, and experience this energy. This energy is then directed into the glass(es) of water.

The rehuna takes up the glass and draws the symbol of Ignizil over it. They should place their dominant hand above the water to direct the energy into it, then drink the water slowly, feeling that energy enter their body. They should focus on how they absorb and experience the energy, how it feels.

The rehuna then imagines that they transform into a

176

shimmery form, for this is how Lunil perceives them, as a being comprised mainly of water.

If the rehuna should wish to, they can direct the energy of Lunil into a particular participant by chanting: ignizil (ig-*ni*-zil). When the power reaches a peak, the energy is directed into the person. This is particularly good if the person concerned needs energy and strength.

Visualisation

Lie or sit comfortably. Close your eyes and breathe deeply for some moments.

See the elemental dehara vegrandis standing at the portals in their quarters. Go now to the west and ask Harudha for permission to enter his realm in the usual fashion. Proceed to Lunil's Nayati, or else invite Lunil to join you in the elemental realm of Harudha.

Now spend some time exploring, and if you wish to, ask Lunil to walk with you there. If there is anything you particularly want to see or learn, ask for these things to be shown to you.

When you are ready, return to normal consciousness.

Dismantling the Nayati

The rehuna should light candles or turn on a soft-light lamp and dismantle the Nayati.

The rehuna stands in the centre, raises arms and says:

> *'Lunil, Dehar of the Moon and of Magic,*
> *Your presence here is always welcome.*
> *I release you from this Nayati*
> *Travel as you will*
> *In this world and all others,*
> *Until our paths cross again,*

In the name of the fifth element,
Aghama, the star and your master,
I bid you farewell.'

The Nayati is then dismantled in the usual manner.

Pelfazzar Majhahn

Pelfazzar was created solely for the purpose of help with financial difficulties. He manifests as a dehar dressed in rich garments, adorned with jewels. He can be seen as leaving golden footprints, or surrounded by glittering motes that continually fell from his body like an aura. He is gaudy, an exaggerated symbol of affluence and plenty.

The Sign of Pelfazzar

As for the seasonal Natalia majhahn, the inclusion of 'play' tools, such as chocolate money and glitter are important. This is to raise the energy of hope in the Nayati, for cares to be banished, for all present to really feel they don't have any financial worries. The idea behind this is that believing it to be true, *utterly* believing it, for just a few moments in the majhahn, a rehuna can affect reality and facilitate the manifestation of a desired potential.

Another important aspect of the majhahn is laughter. If a rehuna should feel ground down by financial concerns, it can affect their entire being with depression and hopelessness. However, once they start laughing during this majhahn, at first self-consciously perhaps, it will just take over, and soon all present will be laughing for real. The atmosphere within the Nayati will dramatically improve, and its energy levels rise: simple laughter can change how a person feels. If a rehuna can laugh in the face of difficulty, they can banish it.

Equipment:

Golden glitter
Gold foil wrapped chocolate money
A candle or tea light (gold or white) for each participant
Wine
Cinnamon flavoured incense or scented oil for burning

The Majhahn

The rehuna creates their Nayati in the usual way, either with the major dehara or the dehara vegrandis in the quarter areas.

The rehuna stands in the centre of the Nayati, facing inwards. They should raise their arms, draw the symbol of Pelfazzar, close their eyes, and first the dehar appearing before them, saying:

'Pelfazzar, Dehar of Abundance, Riches and Plenty
Whose light banishes the shadow of poverty and lack
Whose laughter conjures wealth
Whose smile is golden
Whose footprints shine with diamonds
I call you here this night to empower this work
I call you here to shower upon me the wealth of your being'

Now the rehuna invokes the dehar into the Nayati, with the chant: *'Astale Pelfazzar!'*

When the rehuna has released the power, they should welcome Pelfazzar into the Nayati.

The Visualisation

Prepare as usual for meditation.

See Pelfazzar standing before you. Create your own image of him, a symbol of immense abundance. Imagine that he embraces you, showers you with gifts. Share breath with him, if you wish. Visualise that his breath is golden, that it brings riches to you. His entire being is of wealth and plenty. Being near to him brings these things into your life also. Visualise yourself free of all care to do with money. See yourself fabulously rich, ridiculously so. Let Pelfazzar see how his beneficence will change your life. See yourself laughing, light of being. Really feel what it's like to be released from the survival fears of bad finances.

Conclude the visualisation in the usual way.

The Working

The rehuna now lights their candle, saying something appropriate as to what that action means to them: i.e. 'Here is abundance and richness.' They should cup their hands around the light for a few moments, seeing how the candle flame illumines their skin. They should take that light into themselves.

Now, the rehuna takes up the coins and throws them into the air so that they fall down upon them. If the rehuna is working in ruhahn, all present should throw handfuls of coins at each other. They should be ecstatic and give Pelfazzar an offering of laughter. They should laugh as loud as they can, imagining that the sound of it can change reality. They should laugh madly. They should imagine the coins are real gold.

Then the rehuna eats some of the money. As they unwrap the coin, they should visualise that they are unwrapping a gift from Pelfazzar, a magical food that brings luck and abundance. As they eat it, they should visualise taking that power into themselves. Chocolate is a food of the gods, sumptuous and silky. It represents all good things in life.

Now the rehuna throw handfuls of glitter around. They should utter spontaneously whatever comes to mind, whatever they desire. If working in ruhahn, all should shower each other with the glitter.

The rehuna should close their eyes and imagine this sparkling colour as a magical dust of Pelfazzar. It confers all the riches of life.

If the rehuna so wishes, they may raise power in a chant of their own devising, or do whatever feels right, or has been decided previously to do at this time.

Finally, the rehuna makes a toast to Pelfazzar, either with wine or whatever they wish to drink. If working in ruhahn, all should share a cup, passing it around everyone, and making a toast, as many times as desired.

Dismantling the Nayati

The rehuna stands in the centre, raises arms and says:

> *'Pelfazzar, Dehar of Riches and Gold,*
> *I thank you for your presence and your gifts.*
> *I release you from this Nayati*
> *Travel as you will*
> *In this world and all others,*
> *Until our paths cross again,*
> *In the name of the fifth element,*
> *Aghama, the star and your master,*
> *I bid you farewell.'*

The Nayati is then dismantled in the usual manner.

Deharan Majhahn for Self Knowledge

This majhahn provides a means for furthering self-knowledge with the assistance of the dehara.

To begin, the rehuna sits in the centre of their working space and assumes their majhahn androgynous form.

Once the rehuna feels relaxed and aware, they should call the dehara to them. As they call each one, they should visualise sharing breath with him, imagining that the dehar breathes into them the powers they feel they need to face their innermost self.

The rehuna utters the following invocations, also using the appropriate symbols for each dehar, visualising him appearing and imparting his breath.

> 'Astale Aruhani. Be the firm ground upon which I stand as I face myself.'

> 'Astale Miyacala. Be the clear wind of thought that allows me to truly perceive myself.'

> 'Astale Agave. Be the creative fire that surges through me as I face myself.'

> 'Astale Lunil. Be the water that purifies me as I face myself.'

> 'Astale Aghama. Be the energy that empowers me to know myself.'

At this point if there are other dehara the rehuna wishes to call upon, they should do so.

After the rehuna has called the dehara and has felt their presence, they should lie down and take one hundred deep breaths. They should breathe in through the nose and out through the mouth and as they breathe feel the energy of life circulate within them. Once they've done the hundred breaths, they should take a moment and just feel the silence and within it they will begin to find themselves.

Once this is done, the rehuna visualises a mirror hanging before them. They should look into this mirror. They should look into the eyes of themselves, the windows of the soul, and then speak to themselves. For instance, they could ask why they feel fear of a particular issue. They should make sure to listen to themselves as well, really listen with an open mind and heart. Then, when this is done, they should repeat the process for any other issue that concerns them. Whatever advice is given, they should write it down and then look at it a couple days later and consider it mindfully.

When the rehuna has concluded this procedure, they should ask the dehara for guidance. If the dehara have any messages, these too should be recorded and considered mindfully.

The rehuna then takes a few deep breaths and then brings themselves out of the trance. They should say:

> 'Aruhani, you have bestowed firm ground to stand upon. Depart if you will or stay if you wish.'

> 'Miyacala, you have bestowed the winds of clear thought. Depart as you will or stay if you wish.'

> 'Agave, you have bestowed the creative fire. Depart as you will or stay if you wish.'

> 'Lunil, you have bestowed the purifying water. Depart if you will or stay if you wish.'

> 'Aghama, you have bestowed the energy that empowers me to face the inner self. Depart as you will or stay if you wish.'

A rehuna can modify this majhahn easily. They may call on a specific dehar to aid them in issues associated with health or money. Another way to modify this majhahn is to use incense to create atmosphere (Miyacala), stones for grounding (Aruhani), a lit candle for light (Agave), a cup or bowl of liquid for purification (Lunil). For energy, the rehuna should draw on themselves, since they are energy incarnate. Whatever way helps the rehuna to face themselves, they should use it and be imaginative. They should face what needs to be faced and in doing so free themselves of whatever limitations they've imposed on themselves.

Creating New Dehara

The purpose of creating new dehara is to design entities for specific tasks or influences. Sometimes, during meditation, a new dehar will manifest spontaneously to a rehuna, and it's only after repeated interaction via visualisation that their purpose and meaning become clear. But dehara can also be purposefully designed; either as dehara vegrandis for long-term interaction, or as dehara demitto for a short term task.

The procedure for creating new dehara can be performed by a solitary rehuna or a ruhahn. A ruhahn might wish to create a dehara vegrandis that represents the spirit of their group, and acts as an 'all purpose' dehar for them. Similarly, a solitary rehuna can create a personal dehar for the same reason.

Dehara Vegrandis

The rehuna or ruhahn should decide upon the essence of the desired dehar: its purpose and meaning. They should enter meditation with the express intention of meeting with and forming this dehar. The meditation can be repeated until enough information about the new dehar is built up. During this work, details such as the symbol, appearance, name and epithets of the dehar can be acquired. The rehuna may also devise attributes and a 'history' for the dehar - his own myths

– a festival date, and an etheric realm or palace he inhabits. Details can be received concerning the format of majhahns to the dehar, and what offerings he finds palatable.

Once enough information has been gathered, the rehuna should create a majhahn revolving around the new dehar. During repeated interaction with this entity, the rehuna should continue to programme him as required.

Dehara Demitto

The rehuna creates these entities for specific, short term tasks, such as offering protection during a crisis. Prior to creation, the dehar's purpose and lifespan should be determined, his name and appearance, and also what attributes and powers he will possess.

The rehuna should create their Nayati as usual, and sit within it to meditate. They should create a sigil for their proposed dehar demitto and concentrate upon it. They should call this entity forth from the Source of Creation, naming him as they do so. They should instruct the dehar demitto in whatever task they have set for him. They should inform him of the time limits of this operation.

Should it be required for the lifespan of the dehar demitto to be extended, the rehuna should once again perform a majhahn to do this. They should call the dehar demitto to them and reshape it to their requirements.

This concludes the Grimoire of Kaimana.

Appendix One:
Breathing and Visualisation

Breathing for Meditation

Deep breathing into the stomach helps to alter your state of consciousness, putting you into a meditative state. Before you embark upon any magical operation, a few minutes of purposeful breathing, calms you down and facilitates moving away from mundane reality.

Sit with a straight back, either cross-legged on the floor, on a cushion, or upright on a chair. Let your hands rest loosely in your lap.

Close your eyes and breathe in deeply through the nose for a count of three. As you inhale, push out your stomach and visualise breathing right into your stomach, taking the air all the way down your body.

Hold the breath for a count of three.

Exhale strongly through the mouth for a count of three. As you do so, pull your stomach in again and visualise your body emptying of breath.

Hold again for a count of three, then repeat.

Visualisation

This is a required skill for most magical procedures. Visualisation is like controlled day-dreaming: you imagine pictures in your head, with as much sensory detail as possible. A lot of newcomers to visualisation have difficulty with maintaining the images, or seeing them in any great detail, but as with any other skill, it becomes easier with practice.

To begin visualising, start with simple objects, for which you can imagine more than just the sense of sight, such as a scented flower or a piece of fruit.

Do the breathing exercise for a couple of minutes, and then imagine a black screen before your mind's eye. Upon this screen appears the image of the object you choose to see, for example a rose. Try to see the image in as much detail as you can. What colour is the flower, what shape is it? Try to see the individual petals.

Now imagine picking the flower up in your hands. Run your fingers over the stem. Are there thorns there? Feel the texture of the petals.

Now inhale the scent of the flower. Visualise lifting it to your nose.

You can try this exercise with other objects, such as an apple or orange, so that you can visualise what they taste like too, including the feel of the fruit's texture in your mouth. Try it with objects that make a noise, such as a musical instrument.

If your mind drifts 'off topic', simply refocus your imagination and start from where you left off. People visualise in different ways. You might have a preferred sense, and tend to imagine sounds or voices rather than just 'see' things. You might simply receive impressions.

Once you have mastered visualising simple objects, move on to a living creature, such as a cat. Visualise picking the animal up, stroking its fur.

When you feel confident of being able to hold a visualised image in your mind, begin to experiment with actual scenes, such as walking through an imaginary landscape, such as a forest. Try to engage all your senses: the smells, sounds, and textures around you, as well as the sights. You can begin to populate your visualised environments with creatures and people. You can ride a horse, swim through water, or even fly through the air. Visualise scenes you find interesting, such as an imaginary meeting with someone famous you admire, or a figure from history.

Once you can visualise well, and it's second nature to do it, you'll find that 'inspired' images will come to you. Initially, it might well feel as if you're just making everything up. You are. Even inspired imagery comes from your own inner realm, your imagination. It's the subconscious mind's way of communicating with you, and visualisation is like dreaming while you're awake.

Appendix Two
Creating Sigils and Symbols

Sigils

Sigils can be incorporated into majhahn or as a component of a magari. They are easy to design and are useful for bringing about precise short or long-term results, such as for healing, changing bad habits, dream-control, and other similar operations. Once you have decided upon what your sigil is for, there are various ways of forming it based on that intent. The example below is aimed at people who want to work with the dehara.

"I want to experience Dehara"

1. Mantra - write out intent, as in the above example, and take out any duplicate letters. Scramble the remaining letters into meaningless sentence or word, which can then be chanted. See the example below.

Iwantoexprdh

Possible mantras:

"exto prid whan"
"phran widex to"

2. Monogram - write out your intent, making it as clear and concise as possible. Remove all repeating letters, and from the remaining letters, design a glyph. All the vowels can also be removed. This can then be placed onto a scrap of paper for intense visualisation during meditation or majhahn. See the example below.

Iwantoexprdh – with vowels
Wntxprdh – without vowels

3. Drawing – Using the shape of the letters, you can put them together to draw a picture that represents what you want to happen. You manipulate that picture into a stylised symbol that does not bring the original intent to mind. This can be a simple glyph, or a complex pattern, or swirl similar to Celtic knot work. Also doodling can create some interesting glyphs.

Symbols

During meditation, images might come to you of symbols that have specific meaning to your work. These are not so precisely designed as the sigils described above. You can enter meditation with the intention of finding a symbol.

Another way to create symbols is by automatically drawing them. Take up a pen and in a relaxed state, simply start drawing. Use your whole arm to draw, not just the hand. Make sweeping, free movements. See what you come up with. Different symbols can be combined or adjusted to create the effect you desire.

Appendix Three

Rrakuth Leonis

An Example of Dehar Vegrandis Creation

The feline dehar first appeared to a rehuna one day when she was ill in bed. She visualised a tall dehar with very long fingers and cat-like eyes next to her bed, who performed some kind of healing upon her. We supposed his appearance and attributes were influenced by our work with the Egyptian leonine goddess, Sekhmet – who, as well as being a fiery deity of war and destruction, also has a strong healing aspect. If this was the case with Sekhmet, what would visionary questing into this feline dehar reveal?

The group who worked on this quest consisted of six members, two of whom had not performed any deharan majhahns before, but were enthusiastic to explore the system.

We created a Nayati, and went into a visualisation, asking for this feline dehar to reveal himself and impart some information. The results of this meditation were extremely productive, and the accounts below illustrate what can be achieved when a group of people work together. Some of the accounts are very similar.

Account One:

The dehar's temple was in a sandy, desert area, although I did not pick up a great many details about it. Instead, I concentrated on a dialogue with him. He appeared to me the same as how he had previously been described – with a strong feline ambience and catlike eyes.

He explained to me that one of his functions was to do with the slaying of snakes and scorpions – figuratively as well as literally. Of course, this is a traditional attribute of feline and leonine deities in the Egyptian tradition. It was clear to me from the start that this dehar was strongly associated with the Egyptian frequency, which was not that unusual, given that several members of the participating group had worked with it quite extensively. It didn't surprise me that one of the dehara should have an overtly Egyptian feel to him.

The dehar told me that he could inflict poison as well as draw it. This applied to situations and events as well as people. I could see the usefulness of this attribute in, for example, a situation when there was a lot of bad feeling and misunderstanding. The dehar could be used to 'draw' that poison in the environment, facilitating the restoration of harmony.

He also said that in order to inflict poison, a practitioner should braid their hair before invoking him – or perhaps as part of the majhahn. The braids represented the segmented body of a scorpion.

I had a feeling that this dehar is connected with a dream I'd had over a year before. The dream had been very vivid, and I'd felt at the time it fitted into dehara magic somewhere, but had been unclear as to where and how.

I dreamed of a long blue temple, lined by columns, which overlooked an ocean from high up, as if it was on the side of a cliff. The land beyond seemed Mediterranean in appearance; it probably represented Almagabra. The far end of the temple was open to the elements, enabling me to smell the sea and feel the breeze. The colour blue was unusually prevalent, even in the statues that stood between the columns on either side, and floor beneath my feet. The most unusual thing was that the statues were cat-headed dehara.

There was an opening in the roof, on the left hand side about half way down the room. Steps led up to it. When I investigated this area, I found to my consternation it was some kind of sacrificial ground and that somehar had been ritually slaughtered there. Not a very nice image. It was a square sandy courtyard surrounded by a colonnade, a higher story of the temple beneath. The atmosphere in that place was very different to that of the serene blue area below.

When I awoke from the dream, I thought that my interest in the feline and leonine Egyptian deities must be overlapping or influencing my work with dehara. I couldn't really see how the two things could be melded effectively, without contrivance. However, since the discovery of the feline dehar and the subsequent visualisations during the majhahn we performed, I can see some kind of pattern developing. The two aspects of the dream temple could be symbols for the healing and destructive forms of the cat dehar. Also, the symbolism fits in well with what was originally perceived in visualisation.

Account Two: (from the rehuna who first encountered the dehar)

I was drawn to Agave's realm. In order to reach it, I had to give blood to Agave by cutting my skin (in visualisation). After this, I walked through a wall of flame and down a track surrounded by thick jungle. Suddenly a huge lion confronted me and came towards me. As the lion approached, it changed into the dehar I had seen before in my room. He appeared very tall, with long braided tawny hair and piercing green eyes. His torso was naked and he wore long flowing trousers. His feet were bare. His hands were very slender with bluish green fingernails.

I asked him his name and he said it was Leonis. He opened his palm and an image of two circles intertwining with a pyramid in the middle came from his hand. He did not give

195

any explanation of what this was, or what it could do. We walked along the track and came to a clearing, where I saw a small bamboo hut on a raised dais. As we approached, the doors flung wide with a loud bang!

Inside, it was immense with stairs leading down to a floor from all sides of the hut. Across from us was a huge throne and I enquired whether or not this was Agave's Nayati. Leonis replied that it the temple was his, not Agave's. There appeared to be hara on the floor, with their forearms raised in supplication towards the throne. Leonis just walked through these hara, as if he glided *over* them, and I received the impression that he was not just a healer but something else as well.

Then it was time to go back to reality but I found it hard to come back. Leonis almost seemed to want to keep me in his temple. He had his hands on my shoulders, but I compromised, and said he could come back with me to our physical Nayati and that I would visit him again.

Account Three:

As we sat in the Nayati, me with my back to the west, I was aware of Lunil behind me, touching me on the shoulders. He "lifted" me away, even though I was still aware of my body. I was led through a grey swirling mist, hearing the distinct words, "You are here to observe".

The mists cleared and I saw a golden pyramid with a door in each face, very ornate, although I am hazy on the exact details. At each corner of the pyramid was a large obelisk, made from the same golden stone as the pyramid. They looked similar in structure to Cleopatra's needle, although much larger. It seemed that they reached from earth to the heavens.

Lunil led me inside the pyramid, which initially was dark, until a dais or altar in the very centre of the room began to glow, gently illuminating the room. The altar was rectangular in form and, as I watched, a beam of white light shot up from it and was met by a matching light from some kind of large crystal set in the top of the room. I could now see the whole inside of the structure, which was laid about with sigils and writing a bit like Egyptian hieroglyphs.

Lunil was beside me the whole time. I then saw another figure, tall and slim, with tawny golden skin and a feline sway to his movements. Everything about him was poised and balanced. His face was human, but with a feline cast and his eyes where catlike; a vivid greeny yellow colour. His hair was long and dark, tawny coloured, and plaited into very long fine plaits. His attire reminded me of an Egyptian priest's loincloth and was white, trimmed with gold. He smiled at me. A very confident smile, as if this was his place. Then I was told that I had seen enough for the moment and at that point, we were called back from the meditation.

The rehuna's sketch of Rrakuth Leonis

Account Four:

I did not travel through any of the quarter portals, as my question was asked of the Aghama, and nor was I taken anywhere. But yet I did experience several strong visualisations. The first was before the Nayati was constructed and we heard about our friend's first experience with this new

197

dehar. I became aware of a sigil of some kind and a strong affinity for the colour gold.

While within the Nayati, I was shown a building, this I can only assume was a temple of some kind. It was a grand golden pyramid and set within each side of this structure was a doorway, each doorway was flanked by tall pillar at either side. In total there were four doorways and at the apex of the pyramid, near the top, a single Egyptian-style eye was set – except this eye was that of a cat.

The rehuna's sketch of the temple he saw

The colour was a vibrant green, emerald or jade and it shone with a pure brilliance. As I watched the temple, one door opened and a figure stood within the bright near-white light. This figure was tall; a good head taller than me at over seven feet and its face was beautiful and also feral (a mix between both a beautiful androgyne and a lionesque cat). The dehar's hair was a braided mane of tawny gold hair and it shone with a glimmer the same as the pyramid. The figure's skin was a kind of tanned gold, dusky and perhaps even dusted with a flicker of gold glitter.

The arms were bare, apart from what seemed like golden fire snakes that writhed around and about. The figure's pose suggested a very poised individual and one who knew he was a highly attractive being. His attire was very reminiscent of an Egyptian-style loincloth, again this was almost golden/orange in colour.

Lastly, before I was called back, I became aware of a name: Rrakuth

The figure seemed highly amused and pleased as the temple doors closed and the light faded. Later, as we discussed the other visualisations, I remembered another detail; a strange bracelet of gold, set with three claw-like spikes, the middle was longer than the left and right. It was assumed this was part of a particular majhahn that appeared in other people's visualisations.

I also received a symbol for the dehar, which we all later agreed was associated with the banishing and infliction of poison.

Account Five:

I asked the Aghama to take me to where I needed to go, instead of going to any particular quarter realm. The first thing I was aware of was being surrounded by milky green light. I wandered blindly for what seemed like hours. The only image I was aware of was the shape of a cat's iris and passing through such forms. Then suddenly I found myself in front of a huge set of doors, which opened by themselves. I walked into large temple, bathed in white light, where there was an altar in the centre.

I then had a vision of a very feminine har walking up to the altar and holding out his arms, wrists facing upwards. Out of the light behind the altar came a tall golden figure, who brought down his hands, which while still been harish in form, had long thin metal claws attached on all fingers. The figure sank his claws into the wrists of the har in front of the altar, drawing long streams of blood that fell to the floor. At that point the vision ended and I found myself outside the temple again.

Account Six:

Without having a choice of which quarter to take, I was pulled in to an unknown cave on a cliff side. From the cliff entrance, I could see a jungle or forest below, leading to a beach and vast lake beyond. There was no obvious way out of the cave other than to jump off the cliff, at the cave entrance. After jumping, I plummeted quickly and slowed as the ground came closer, and landed softly.

I was drawn towards the beach area, so I followed a path through the forest, until I came to a granite oblong stone upright in the ground. The stone was carved with intricate patterns, and had convex front, on the centre a circular groove was carved out. In the centre of this circle was a small hole about two inches in diameter, which was bleeding. But the pull of the beach dragged me on.

When I arrived at the beach, I was drawn towards the water's edge. When I looked into it, I saw a stylised portrait of myself. Knowing this was not me, I concentrated on the image and saw the 'real' me.

I then walked across the beach, and towards what looked like a Canada Lynx, but as I approached, a haze cleared, and I could see a golden figure standing there, wearing a strange necklace. As I approached, I could see the figure more clearly and could tell it knew what I was coming for. We communicated without speaking, and he showed me the

 necklace, and said this is my symbol. After seeing the false image of myself in the water, I had a feeling there was deception a foot. So I forcefully said 'No! Show me the real symbol.' The figure replied 'Look in to the sky, the clouds have your answer.' There I saw the symbol for the Dehar, which is used in his invocation.

Appendix Four
The Birth of Kiraziel,
Dehar of Realised Dreams

The previous example illustrated one way of creating dehara. Kiraziel, the subject of this section, is another new dehar that was created by Taylor Ellwood. Taylor explains his work in his own words.

'This majhahn began around mid-October 2003. Storm and I had talked about the idea of a dehar who manifested realities, and helped people realise their dreams. I decided to take an unusual approach to this, in that I would create the dehar as if it had been created through the sexual union of har with har. The idea of this was also to make this dehar mortal, so that he could understand what it was to be mortal, to have needs and wants and fears.

'For the first part of this majhahn, I used the gateway majhahn to meet my harish self and explained to him what I wanted to do. The way I perceive it, there are countless versions of ourselves, and if we are willing to believe in the reality depicted by a series of books, then a version of ourselves exists in that reality. The Aghama played a role in this, in that he was the creator of the pearl, whilst my harish self was the hostling.

'The colour of the pearl we created was black. For approximately a week, I did the Gateway majhahn and visited my harish self. I put energy into the pearl, as well as a name: Kiraziel. The name had been told to me by the Aghama.

'Once the pearl cracked, the next part of the majhahn began. This consisted of doing the Gateway majhahn each night from the end of October until Yule. The idea behind this was to familiarise Kiraziel with my self and my needs, what it was I wanted him to help me manifest into reality. The work was interesting, because what I learned about Kiraziel was that he has the ability to perceive all the probabilities surrounding your desires. He suggested to me things I could do to help manifest desires into reality. The repeated Gateway majhahns attuned him to me and my needs. I think the length of time you devote to this would vary with the intensity of your needs, and also how able you are to manifest those needs into reality by yourself.

'For the solstice majhahn, Maryam (my partner) and I decided to do sex magick to give Kiraziel his Feybraiha, and in the process begin the actual magickal work he'd do to manifest my desires into reality. Feybraiha is the rite of passage from childhood to adulthood, when a har becomes sexually active. We laid out our stone eggs to create a circle. At the beginning, all three of our cats were in the circle. I painted on myself sigils of the dehara, including that of Kiraziel, who that night had had his Feybraiha majhahn and thus had become a dehar. Kiraziel's sigil is interesting because when you do it you actually combine it with your own sigil, so his sigil will be different for each person who works with him. I called on each of the dehara and then Maryam and I explained our purposes for doing the majhahn. Our purposes were directed to Kiraziel, who is the dehar that manifests wishes into reality. I called Kiraziel into me. We felt the other dehara stand around us. The cats left the circle. Maryam and I ritually enacted the Feybraiha of Kiraziel. We remained motionless for the most part, practicing a Tantric technique where you move as little as possible, but let your body take over. There was no physical orgasm, but rather a spiritual one where we again voiced our needs to Kiraziel and in response he used the energy of the act to begin the manifestation of those needs into reality. Maryam said she saw Kiraziel in me and I felt him as well. For a while I was present, but not doing anything, allowing him to take control and have his feybraiha through me. Both Maryam and I noted some intriguing phenomena as this occurred. First our faces looked both male and female and then we noted that each other's face shifted, changing shape. My impression of Kiraziel as a dehar is a long silver haired, azure-eyed dehar with very pale skin. He told me that he was the Dehar of Many Within One. What this means is that while he is one dehar he represents the many desires of those who call on him to help manifest reality. So he becomes many different versions of himself to fulfil those desires. He is different from the other Dehara in that he is mortal. When a wish is manifested by him, that part which did it dies and returns to him. He lives through the cycle of life and death to understand those who call on him and their needs. You do not need to use sex magick to call on him. All you need is the desire and a willingness to do a majhahn of his/her choice that explains the need to Kiraziel.'

Resources

Books

Creating Magical Entities, Taylor Ellwood
*Pop Culture Magick, Taylor Ellwood
Oven Ready Chaos, Phil Hine
Prime Chaos, Phil Hine
*The Enchantments of Flesh and Spirit, Storm Constantine
*The Bewitchments of Love and Hate, Storm Constantine
*The Fulfilments of Fate and Desire, Storm Constantine
*The Wraiths of Will and Pleasure, Storm Constantine
*The Shades of Time and Memory, Storm Constantine
*The Ghosts of Blood and Innocence, Storm Constantine
*The Hienama, Storm Constantine
*Student of Kyme, Storm Constantine
*Sekhem Heka, Storm Constantine

Music

Steve Roach, The Magnificent Void
Steve Roach, Serpent's Lair
Synaesthesia, Ephemeral

*Available as Immanion Press titles. See web site for details.
http://www.immanion-press.com

Glossary

Acantha	The first level of the Ulani tier
Acanthalid	A rehuna of Acantha level
Adkaya	The majhahn performed two weeks before Natalia, when Solarisel gives for the pearl of Elisin
Agave	One of the major dehara, associated with fire, intention, healing, protection and aggression.
Aghama	the dehar associated with the centre of a Nayati, spirit
Agmara	The life-giving energy of the universe
Aislinn	A level of the Nahir Nuri tier
Algoma	Third level of the Ulani tier
Algomalid	A rehuna of Algoma level
Aloyt	The dehar of dreams
Ara	First level of the Kaimana tier
Aralid	A rehuna of Ara level
Arojhahn	A seasonal festival
Arotahar	The cycle of the seasons
Aruhani	major dehar, associated with aruna (sex), life and death. Both creator and destroyer.
Aruna	Sexual activity between two hara
Astale	A term used to invoke dehara

Auracas	The elemental palace of Fire
Avatar of Beauty	An epithet of the Aghama
Beautiful One, The	An epithet of Aruhani
Beauty of Life	An epithet of Elisin
Beauty of Nature	An epithet of Morterrius
Bloomtide	An arojhahn held on 1st February
Blue Flame	An epithet of Lunil
Brynie	Third level of the Kaimana tier
Brynielid	A rehuna of Brynie level
Chamber of Gateways	A visualised portal to imaginary realms
Child of Light	An epithet of Elisin
Cleatha	A level of the Nahir Nuri tier
Cuttingtide	An arojhahn held at the summer solstice
Dark One	An epithet of Aruhani
Dehar	An androgynous deity
Dehar of Abundance, Riches and Plenty	An epithet of Pelfazzar
Dehar of Air	An epithet of Naivedya
Dehar of Aruna, Life and Death	An epithet of Aruhani
Dehar of Azure Light	An epithet of Lunil
Dehar of Darkness and Fire	An epithet of Lachrymide
Dehar of Dreams	An epithet of Aloyt
Dehar of Earth	An epithet of Phorlakh
Dehar of Fire	An epithet of Elauria
Dehar of Initiation, Knowledge & Inspiration	An epithet of Miyacala
Dehar of Plenty	An epithet of Prosperiel
Dehar of Plenty and Abundance	An epithet of Prosperiel
Dehar of Promise	An epithet of Prosperiel
Dehar of Riches and Gold	An epithet of Pelfazzar
Dehar of Shadows	An epithet of Lachrymide
Dehar of Silver Light	An epithet of Lunil
Dehar of the Elemental East	An epithet of Naivedya

Dehar of the Elemental North	An epithet of Phorlakh
Dehar of the Elemental South	An epithet of Elauria
Dehar of the Elemental West	An epithet of Harudha
Dehar of Knowledge and Initiation	An epithet of Miyacala
Dehar of the Light's Potential	An epithet of Solarisel
Dehar of the Moon and of Magic	An epithet of Lunil
Dehar of the Mysteries of Aruna, Life and Death	An epithet of Aruhani
Dehar of the Mysteries of the Moon and of Magic	An epithet of Lunil
Dehar of the Sacred Fire	An epithet of Agave
Dehar of Ultimate Potential	An epithet of Miyacala
Dehar of Water	An epithet of Harudha
Dehara	Plural form of dehar
Dehara Demitto	Dehara created by the rehuna for temporary magical purposes
Dehara Vegrandis	Permanent dehara, lower in status than the 5 major dehara
Deharling	A young dehar
Devourer	An epithet of Aruhani
Dryalimah	The dehara term for the Tree of Life
Eburniel	A dehar associated with Rosatide
Efrata	A level of the Nahir Nuri tier
Elauria	Elemental dehar of Fire
Elisin	A dehar of Arotahar, the Child of Light
Eviya	The area on the body, behind the navel, where the rehuna visualises their life force residing
Fayganza	Elemental Palace of Water
Feyrahni	A dehar associated with Feybraihatide
Feybraihatide	An arojhahn held on 1st May

Field Walker	An epithet of Verdiferel
Florinel	A dehar associated with Bloomtide
Fholids	Deharan elementals of Earth
Flimmerids	Elemental creatures of Fire
Forest of Ijhimere	Mythical location of Oorn, the Palace of Earth
Guardian of Arotahar	An epithet applied to all seasonal dehara
Guardian of the Inner Ways	An epithet of Lunil
Halo of Agmara	A visualised circle of protective energy
Halo of Power	A visualised circle of protective energy
Har (hara)	Imaginary androgynous beings, intrinsic to the world of dehara.
Harhune	A rite of initiation, whereby a rehuna visualises acquiring a ritual androgynous form
Harudha	Elemental dehar of Water
He and She in One	An epithet of Agave
He Who Sees Beyond the Veil	An epithet of Lachrymide
He Who Walks the Furrows in Darkness	An epithet of Shadolan
He Whose Body is the Sky	An epithet of Aruhani
Heart of the Lengthening Days	An epithet of Elisin
Heart of the Shortening Days	An epithet for Prosperiel
Hienama	A magical teacher, created and visualised by a rehuna
Hienama of the Spheres	An epithet of Lunil
Hostling	A har or dehar who carries a pearl and gives birth to it
Hostling and Protector of all Future Hope	An epithet of Solarisel
Hostling of Bones	An epithet of Aruhani
Hostling of the Pearl of Hope	An epithet of Lachrymide
Igniteran	The etheric Nayati of Agave
Ignizil	A form of agmara energy

	associated with Lunil
Julangis	The etheric Nayati of Aruhani
Kaimana	The first tier of the Dehara magical caste system
Kirazael	Dehar of realised dreams
Lachrymide	A dehar associated with Shadetide
Life of the Land	An epithet of Morterrius
Loraylah	The etheric Nayati of Lunil
Lord of the Cosmos	An epithet of the Aghama
Lord of the Forest Ways	An epithet of Florinel
Lord of the Libraries of the Cosmos	An epithet for Miyacala
Lord of the Secret Glades	An epithet of Feyrahni
Lunil	One of the major dehara, associated with magic, intuition, and the moon
Magari	A short magical working, a spell
Majhahn	A magical ritual
Miyacala	One of the major dehara, associated with initiation, knowledge and inspiration
Morterrius	A dehar associated with Cuttingtide
Nahir Nuri	The third tier of the Dehara magical caste system
Naivedya	The elemental dehar of Air
Natalia	An arojhahn held at the winter solstice, Dec 21st
Nayati	A temple or ritual space
Neoma	Second level in Kaimana
Neomalid	A rehuna of Neoma level
Oorn	The elemental Palace of Earth
Otherlanes, The	Visualised pathways between etheric realms
Ouana-lim	The masculine generative organs of a har
Ozaril	An energy sometimes

	manifested by Verdiferel
Panphilien	A dehar who embodies all the separate dehara of Arotahar
Pazini	Elemental creatures of Air
Pelfazzar	Dehar of abundance and riches
Phantom of the Corn	An epithet of Verdiferel
Phorlakh	The elemental dehar of Earth
Prosperiel	A dehar associated with Smoketide
Protector, Warrior and Healer	An epithet of Agave
Pyralis	The second level of the Ulani tier
Pyralisit	A rehuna of Pyralis level
Reaptide	An arojhahn held on 1st August
Rehuna	The term for any person working with Dehara
Rosatide	An arojhahn held on 1st February
Rrakuth Leonis	Dehar of healing and poisons
Ruhahn	The term for a group of rehunas working together
Samuntala	Etheric Nayati of the Aghama
Sedu	A visualised creature that can negotiate the otherlanes
Shaddari	Elemental creatures of Water
Shadetide	An arojhahn held on October 31st
Shadolan	A dehar associated with Cuttingtide
Shadowpeak	A mythical mountain at the heart of the world, location of Shuraya
Sharing Breath	An act between hara or dehara whereby information, images and feelings are transmitted intimately through the breath.

Shayyai	Burning lamps used for majhahn
Shuraya	The elemental palace of Air
Smoketide	An arojhahn held on the Autumn Equinox, Sept 21st
Solarisel	A dehar associated with Adkaya and Natalia
Soume-lam	Feminine generative organs of a har
Spirit of the of the Noontide of Ghosts	An epithet of Verdiferel
Tahanica	The Etheric Nayati of Miyacala
Thiede	A name for the Aghama when he appears in harish form
Tigron of the Spheres	An epithet of the Aghama
Ulani	The second tier of the Dehara magical caste system
Vakei	A ritual blade used in majhahn
Verdiferel	A dehar associated with Reaptide
Walker of Battlefields	An epithet of Agave
Walker of the Furrows	An epithet of Shadolan
Walker Upon the North Star Road	An epithet of Miyacala
Warrior of Eternal Fire, The	An epithet of Agave
White Walker of the Fields	An epithet of Eburniel
Wraeththu	A fictional race of hermaphroditic magical beings